HEYDAYS

at The June Motel

Welcome to
SAUBLE BEACH

HEYDAYS

at The June Motel

BEACH TOWN CLASSICS

FREDDY LALIBERTÉ *and* EVAN BAULCH
WITH KATIE LALIBERTÉ *and* EMMA BAULCH

Foreword by
APRIL BROWN *and* SARAH SKLASH

PHOTOGRAPHY BY LAUREN MILLER

AMBROSIA

Heydays

Published in Canada in 2024 and the USA in 2024 by House of Anansi Press Inc.
houseofanansi.com

House of Anansi Press is committed to protecting our natural environment. This book is made of material from well-managed FSC®-certified forests, recycled materials, and other controlled sources.

House of Anansi Press is a Global Certified Accessible™ (GCA by Benetech) publisher. The ebook version of this book meets stringent accessibility standards and is available to readers with print disabilities.

28 27 26 25 24 1 2 3 4 5

Library and Archives Canada Cataloguing in Publication

Title: Heydays at The June Motel : beach town classics / Freddy Laliberté and Evan Baulch; with Katie Laliberté and Emma Baulch; foreword by April Brown and Sarah Sklash; photography by Lauren Miller.

Names: Laliberté, Freddy, author. | Baulch, Evan, author. | Laliberté, Katie, author. | Baulch, Emma, author. | Brown, April (Co-founder of The June Motel), writer of foreword. | Sklash, Sarah, writer of foreword. | Miller, Lauren (Photographer), photographer.

Description: Includes index.

Identifiers: Canadiana (print) 2023062202X | Canadiana (ebook) 20230622038
ISBN 9781487011642 (hardcover) | ISBN 9781487011659 (EPUB)
Subjects: LCSH: Heydays (Restaurant) | LCSH: Cooking—Ontario—Sauble Beach.
LCSH: Comfort food. | LCSH: Cooking. | LCGFT: Cookbooks.
Classification: LCC TX714 .L343 2024 | DDC 641.5—dc23

Book design: Greg Tabor
Cover and interior photography: Lauren Miller
Photo on page 130 (Motel Makeover) by Darren Goldstein courtesy of Proper Television;
photos on pages 155 and 157 (Parking Lot Pop-Up) courtesy of Sarah Sklash;
photo on page 181 (Evan with paella) courtesy of April Brown.

House of Anansi Press is grateful for the privilege to work on and create from the Traditional Territory of many Nations, including the Anishinabeg, the Wendat, and the Haudenosaunee, as well as the Treaty Lands of the Mississaugas of the Credit.

Canada Council for the Arts | Conseil des Arts du Canada | ONTARIO ARTS COUNCIL CONSEIL DES ARTS DE L'ONTARIO

With the participation of the Government of Canada
Avec la participation du gouvernement du Canada | Canada

We acknowledge for their financial support of our publishing program the Canada Council for the Arts, the Ontario Arts Council, and the Government of Canada.

Printed and bound in Canada

For our children,
the most discerning of food critics

Contents

Foreword

We distinctly remember the first time we ate a meal at Heydays. It was early July, when our little town of Sauble Beach, Ontario, was coming alive for the season. A warm golden light bathed the patio as the sun was setting and we sipped on our cold glasses of rosé—a magnum chilling tableside—as one does at Heydays. We had fifty oysters for the table, and hot buttered lobster rolls were on their way. In that moment we were living our best lives, creating the kind of memories summer is for. And we were dining in the middle of a ... parking lot. Yes, a parking lot.

It was still all-renovation all-day at The June Motel and Heydays that week, but Evan and Freddy wanted to be doing what they do best: making delicious food. So at the beginning of summer, when cottagers started flooding the area, these guys scrubbed down the kitchen, ordered picnic tables, fired up the flat top, and created a pop-up restaurant in the middle of the Heydays parking lot.

Together with our friends, we worked our way through that magnum of rosé and experienced our very first Heydays lobster roll. We marvelled at how the patio had been a mere parking lot just that morning and now was on its way to being the hottest restaurant in Sauble Beach.

It was definitely a vibe, and the food was transformative. While we were determined to create a beautiful and Insta-worthy restaurant for the Heydays crew to serve their food, it was clear they didn't need it. The food spoke for itself. It was casual but trendy, simple but indulgent, summery but comforting.

Since that first dining experience, we've collectively eaten at Heydays more than a hundred times. When we're working at The June in Sauble Beach, we make it our mission to eat our way through the entire menu—smash burgers, fried chicken, broccoli Caesar salads, and many, many lobster rolls. And when we're not at The June, we dream about what we'll order on our next visit. Some might call it an obsession, but we like to say it's a commitment to quality control.

To us, summer has become synonymous with eating delicious food at Heydays. It's frosé and smash burgers poolside for lunch in the sunshine, and magical dinners under twinkling string lights, eating good food and drinking good wine with friends. At its core, that is what Heydays is all about. It's a place for our guests and locals to come together and live the good life—where wine is poured, stories are shared, and food is enjoyed.

If we've learned anything from dining at Heydays, it's that good food can create great memories. While many will experience the good life first-hand by dining at Heydays, we believe these recipes deserve to be shared so they can be recreated in your kitchen, served at your table, and enjoyed with your people.

April Brown & Sarah Sklash
Co-founders, The June Motel

WELCOME TO Heydays

SOMEDAY, THESE WILL BE THE GOOD OLD DAYS ...

At Heydays, we know our guests are here to celebrate. It could be an anniversary or birthday, or a Saturday night, or 3 p.m. on a Monday in the middle of summer. Whenever it is, our guests are here to make memories. When we designed our first menu, we kept the idea of celebration in mind. We included simple dishes and comfort foods that diners expect from a classic beach town restaurant, but we worked to make them the best versions we'd ever tasted.

Heydays fits naturally into the small town of Sauble Beach on the eastern shore of Lake Huron—a place that oozes history and has an air of nostalgia for bygone times. We wanted to ensure that our menu was filled with classic dishes and cocktails that would transport our guests far away from the hassles of everyday life. We drew on some of our favourite memories: celebration dinners at a classic steakhouse, barefoot visits to dockside lobster shacks, the unceasing quality of a classic French bistro, and the poolside casualness of a potluck barbecue. While these might seem like very different experiences, they can all be found at a seat on our patio. It just depends on what you order.

The restaurant team consists of two families: the Lalibertés and the Baulches. Freddy and Evan have deep backgrounds building restaurants, both together and separately. They met at university, where they helped to bring a local fine-dining restaurant to life. Freddy went on to create successful casual comfort food concepts in Toronto (high-quality poutine and mac and cheese), and Evan managed some of Canada's top restaurants and properties. Their combined experience—both casual and high-end—as well as their technical attention to quality and dedication to beautiful presentation resulted in the Heydays menu that so many regular customers and guests of The June Motel have come to love. Heydays is a collaboration between the kitchen crew and the team that founded The June Motel. Freddy and Evan created the menu and oversee operations at the restaurant, while April and Sarah shaped the brand to fit with The June Motel in Sauble Beach.

Together, we did a lot of recipe testing in the lead-up to summer 2020, when Heydays first opened. We learned what made our own meals feel special, and then we brought them to the restaurant, whether it was a parking lot pop-up or the beautiful poolside patio that Sarah and April built for us.

This book will take you through a night on our patio. We'll start with sunset cocktails, then serve a delicious seafood platter, and follow that up with some smoked trout fishcakes, potato cheddar croquettes, and a salad or two (definitely the broccoli Caesar). Then you'll have to try a hot buttered lobster roll, a crispy skin trout, our signature steak, and seasonal vegetable sides. Finish it off with our sweet, savoury desserts: a "key" lime parfait and an ice cream sundae with Grandmaman's oats. It might sound like a lot, but you can share and try it all!

Because these recipes began their lives at home (in the middle of a pandemic, no less), we know they'll translate well from our restaurant to your kitchen. And whether you've joined us at Heydays before or not, we hope that you'll taste something of the poolside life in every dish. We also hope that by enjoying our favourite dishes at home, you'll be inspired to come celebrate with us in Sauble Beach when you're able.

Bevvies

It's magic hour on the Heydays patio. The sky is starting to glow pink as the sun takes its daily dip into the blue waters of Lake Huron. It's still warm enough that the pool is busy, and the music is just right. It is most certainly time for a cocktail. Because, as we say around here, it would be rude not to.

Bevvies come first because we think that's how entertaining should go. First, we welcome you to our restaurant, and then we might ask you about your day at the beach or by the pool. Don't think about food yet. For now, enjoy magic hour, bevvy in hand.

There is something about the classic cocktail that feels like an instant escape. When we started building our Heydays cocktail menu, we first thought about what we wanted to taste, both poolside and on the patio. Next, we thought about cocktails that we'd be able to batch for easy service, making them ideal for home entertaining, too. You might be familiar with a number of these cocktails, and they're fairly simple for the most part. We've included them here as a reminder when you're thinking about a fun way to welcome guests into your home.

BEVVIES

About Rosé

Rosé wine was an important part of The June Motel story long before Heydays was around. At The June Motel, it is tradition to welcome guests into the Lobby Bar with a crisp glass of rosé. It signals vacation time and also looks beautiful against the pink doors of the motel rooms. Rosé is an integral part of The June Motel experience. Since we certainly like wine, it wasn't hard to ensure that The June Motel's rosé moment was echoed through the restaurant as well.

While there are different ways of making rosé, it is usually the result of removing the dark grape skins from the aging process, whereas red wines would keep them. Having some contact with the skins results in a tannin content that allows rosé to pair nicely with a wide range of food. Tannins are the mouth-puckering element in wine that can help cut through fats and enhance flavours.

We love our Canadian rosés, and we also have a predilection for dry, savoury French rosés that border on rose gold in colour. We like rosés that might be more appropriately characterized as "orange" with their skin contact and funkiness. We like bubbly rosé, and perhaps, in the most Heydays tradition, we even like rosé in slushy machines (see our DIY Frosé on page 22).

One of our favourite parts of our parking lot patio restaurant (see page 155) was watching long-time regulars of the previous motel's restaurant elevate frosé to an instant classic.

While rosé seems to be having a moment, it is actually thought to be the oldest type of wine, given that the practice of allowing skin contact dates back through the history of winemaking. It got a bit of a bad rap in North America following the popularity of the saccharine white Zinfandel, which seemed to lack the sophistication of its old-world counterparts, but North American rosés have come a long way since the 1980s, so we like to mix it up.

We find our rosés to be a great accompaniment to just about everything on our menu, from the Seafood Platter (page 30) to our Striploin with Confit Garlic (page 161) to our Charred Broccoli Caesar (page 85).

Lemon-Leftover Lemonade

If you've followed our lemon-cutting tutorial (page 43) and have prepared a Heydays-style feast that starts with a Seafood Platter (page 30), you will likely have some leftover "lemon guts"—the lemon core that's left behind when you cut a lot of lemon garnish the Heydays way. Save them! They make a great lemonade. At the restaurant, we put our lemonade in a slushie machine to make it the perfect poolside accompaniment. You can blend it up with ice to replicate at home.

TO MAKE A PITCHER OF LEMONADE (8 CUPS/2 L)

2 cups (500 mL) freshly squeezed and strained lemon juice (8 to 10 whole lemons)
2 cups (500 mL) simple syrup (see Heydays Tip)
4 cups (1 L) cold water

1 Combine the lemon juice, simple syrup, and cold water in a large pitcher. Stir. Chill.

TO MAKE 2 GLASSES OF FROZEN LEMONADE

2 cups (500 mL) ice
2 cups (500 mL) prepared lemonade (see recipe above)

1 Combine the ice and prepared lemonade in a blender. Starting on low and gradually increasing to high speed, blend until the ice is homogeneous with the lemonade.

2 Divide the frozen lemonade between two glasses. Add straws. Sip. Enjoy!

Heydays Tip

We prep simple syrup in advance and then keep it in the fridge for up to 2 weeks. We like to boil water in a kettle and pour 1¼ cups (300 mL) boiling water over 1¼ cups (300 mL) granulated or demerara sugar in a large heat-safe glass measuring cup, keeping it covered while the sugar dissolves. Give it a good stir and cool completely before refrigerating.

Sauble Beach Lemonade (SBL)

This cocktail was inspired by a staple at one of our favourite summer town beach bars, a great dive bar with a cold beverage bubbler that was perpetually full of boozy lemonade. You have to be a little careful with this one, as the alcohol flavour is completely camouflaged by lemon and sugar.

If you've already got the blender out, adding the liquor to your slushy lemonade is probably the best way to go, but you can also do it the way we do, by dumping shots of booze over frozen lemonade and recommending that your guests stir vigorously.

MAKES 1 COCKTAIL

1¼ oz (35 mL) Jameson Irish Whiskey
1¼ oz (35 mL) French brandy
12 oz (355 mL) Lemon-Leftover Lemonade (page 10)

1. If using the non-frozen pitcher of Lemon-Leftover Lemonade, add a scoop of ice to a glass. Pour the whiskey and brandy into the glass. Top with lemonade. We recommend vigorous stirring.

2. If you want frozen SBLs (like we serve at Heydays), you can add the whiskey and brandy right to the blender, using these quantities as a guide. Enjoy!

Heydays Tip

Make-ahead: Combine the whiskey and brandy ahead of time so all you have to do when company arrives is pour 2½ oz (75 mL) of the mix into the lemonade.

PEACE LOVE ROSÉ

Aperol Spritz

Even though there's a recipe right there on the Aperol bottle, the "correct" ratio of Aperol to sparkling wine has provoked a surprising number of opinions. We prefer a lighter dose of Aperol paired with Cava, a sparkling wine made in Spain. The case could be made that it would be more appropriate to pair Aperol, an Italian spirit, with Prosecco, but we happen to like Cava. So we put lots of it in our spritz and top with a bit of sparkling water.

MAKES 1 COCKTAIL

1½ oz (45 mL) Aperol
4 oz (120 mL) Cava
1½ oz (45 mL) sparkling water
Orange wheels, cut in half, for garnish

1. We serve our Aperol Spritz in a wine glass filled with ice. First, add the Aperol. Then slowly (so it doesn't foam up too much) pour in the Cava. Top with the sparkling water. Garnish each glass with a half orange wheel.

2. You should end up with a gorgeous ombré cocktail, but encourage guests to give it a stir before drinking or their first sip will be a saccharine hit of Aperol.

Negroni

The Negroni is a simple classic cocktail and you might even know the recipe already. We include it here because it is one of our favourite patio aperitivos—simple and balanced, perfect all year round. If you're prepping for a cocktail party, batch them using one whole bottle of each spirit, just remember to make sure that all your bottles are the same size! We learned this lesson the hard way.

MAKES 1 COCKTAIL

1 oz (30 mL) gin
1 oz (30 mL) Campari
1 oz (30 mL) red vermouth (Dolin is delicious—try it on its own, over ice, and garnished with a lemon slice)
Orange peel, for garnish

1. In a cocktail pitcher, combine the gin, Campari, and red vermouth, and then add a scoop of ice. Use a long cocktail spoon to stir everything together—the swishing over ice not only cools the cocktail but also adds just a bit of dilution that is crucial to a delicious Negroni.

2. Using a Hawthorne strainer, strain over a king cube in a rocks glass. (King cubes are large square cubes that add a little class to cocktails.) You can also serve this cocktail neat, strained into a champagne coupe.

3. Finish by twisting an orange peel over the glass to release its oil, and then glide the peel around the glass rim so every sip has an orange essence.

Old Fashioned

Call us old fashioned, but we love a good bourbon cocktail (see what we did there?). Maybe it's just that *Mad Men* is still living rent-free in our heads, but the vintage nostalgic flavour of this strong yet balanced cocktail gets us right in the feels. This is a great way to finish a meal, but it also goes beautifully with Marinated Warm Olives (page 211) at cocktail hour.

MAKES 1 COCKTAIL

2 oz (60 mL) bourbon
5 dashes of Angostura bitters
1 bar spoon (1/4 oz/5 mL) demerara sugar simple syrup (page 10)
Orange peel, for garnish

1. Fill a mixing carafe or cocktail shaker with ice. Add the bourbon, Angostura, and simple syrup. Stir for 20 seconds.

2. Using a Hawthorne strainer, strain into a rocks glass over a king cube.

3. Garnish with an orange peel. This cocktail is best enjoyed alongside olives and deep thoughts.

Sbagliato

Pronounced *zba-yee-ah-toe* (the Italian "gli" makes a "y" sound), this cocktail is a Negroni topped with sparkling wine. You might have seen this coming, but we use Cava, even if that's, once again, mixing our Italian and Spanish alcohols. It's a refreshing way to lengthen the Negroni experience. Classically there is no gin in a sbagliato, but we don't care: sometimes it's nice to have a Negroni batched and queued that can then be easily turned into a sbagliato.

MAKES 1 COCKTAIL

1 oz (30 mL) gin
1 oz (30 mL) Campari
1 oz (30 mL) red vermouth
3 oz (90 mL) Cava
Orange peel, for garnish

1. In a cocktail pitcher, combine the gin, Campari, and red vermouth, and then add a scoop of ice. Stir everything together with a cocktail spoon.
2. Using a Hawthorne strainer, strain into either a rocks glass with a king cube or a coupe glass without ice. Top with Cava.
3. Finish by twisting an orange peel over the glass.

Heydays Rum Punch

The flavour of this juicy rum punch brings us back to the New England golf course we worked at years ago. From-concentrate orange juice is essential to this recipe. It tends to be a little sweeter and goes well with the rum in this cocktail. We recommend making a big batch of rum punch and serving it by the pool on a hot summer day.

SERVES 12

8 cups (2 L) orange juice from concentrate
23 oz (680 mL) pineapple juice (half a standard 46 oz/1.36 L can)
25.4 oz (750 mL) bottle white rum
1 oz (30 mL) grenadine
Dark rum float, to taste (see Heydays Tip)

1. In a large jug or punch bowl, combine the orange juice, pineapple juice, white rum, and grenadine.

2. Fill a highball glass with ice. Add 8 oz (240 mL) of the punch mix and ½ oz (15 mL) of dark rum as a float. To ensure that you get a nice dark rum layer on top, pour the rum over the back of a spoon. Garnish with a cherry and orange slice held together with a small bamboo skewer. Add a straw, sip, and enjoy.

Heydays Tip

For a little boozy fun and pretty finish, we sometimes like to add a "float" to our cocktails, using liquor that is a complementary colour and flavour. For our Rum Punch, pouring about ½ oz (15 mL) of dark rum overtop gives the drink an ombré look. We free pour gently for this effect, but you can also pour the rum over the back of a spoon to get a more defined layer.

DIY *Frosé*

At Heydays, we have the benefit of two slushie machines to ensure that both our bars are well stocked with frosé and frozen lemonade.

That said, we've done some experimenting to recreate the Heydays frosé experience at home sans slushie machine! Unlike some other frosés on the market, ours is simple: We don't add extra sugar or booze; we just pour wine into the slushie machine and serve it. It helps to have a wine that already has a bit of sweetness to it. We use a Canadian rosé that has 29 grams of sugar per litre. By comparison, some of those French "rose gold" rosés have only 2 grams of sugar per litre. Don't use your nice expensive rosés on frosé; boxed wine will do just fine.

MAKES 2 SERVINGS OF FROSÉ PER ICE CUBE TRAY

1. For a round of home frosés, fill a few ice cube trays with rosé wine. Ice cubes are about 1 oz (30 mL) of liquid each, so one tray will give you about two decent portions of frosé. Let the trays freeze overnight.

2. Empty the trays of ice into a blender just before serving. Give the frozen rosé "blobs" a quick blitz, once or twice, just until they reach a pourable consistency.

3. Pour your frosés into a round of wine glasses and enjoy by the pool.

SOMEDAY,
THESE WILL
BE THE GOOD

Mimosa

Our season starts at Mother's Day with a very busy brunch. We serve so many mimosas that day that we've considered permanently changing the name to *momosa*. Okay, that's cheesy, but it gets some laughs even when seven tables are waiting for a fresh pot of coffee to brew. While it can be nice to have fresh squeezed orange juice, we love frozen concentrate orange juice in cocktails for a number of reasons: 1) it tastes great with booze of all kinds, 2) it offers consistency in flavour; and 3) you can always keep it in your freezer for emergency mimosas. Ensure your orange juice and Cava are cold before starting. Flutes are a pain to wash, so we serve mimosas in a wine glass with no ice.

MAKES 1 COCKTAIL

5 oz (150 mL) Cava
1 oz (30 mL) orange juice from concentrate

1 Fill your wine glass with the Cava, and then pour the orange juice overtop. Enjoy!

Bloody Mary

Much of our menu was inspired by New England coastal resort menus, so we debated long and hard about whether to serve a horseradish Bloody Mary or its traditional Canadian Clamato-based cousin, the Caesar. We split the difference and put a Bloody Caesar on the menu and now everybody's confused! But that's fine, because we can usually tell that someone needs one before they even grope around the menu looking for it. Prepared horseradish is just fine, but we really like shaved fresh horseradish for the extra kick. Here's our take on the Classic Bloody Mary. If you're game for Clamato, try the Caesar, too! You can substitute your spirit of choice in this one—we were on a Bacardi Limon Rum kick for a little while.

MAKES 1 COCKTAIL

Old Bay Seasoning, for rim
Lemon and lime wedges, for rim and garnish
3 dashes of Worcestershire sauce
1 tsp (5 mL) fresh lemon juice
1 dash of hot sauce
1 tbsp (15 mL) prepared horseradish
Pinch of sea salt
Pinch of freshly ground black pepper
2 oz (60 mL) vodka
6 oz (180 mL) tomato juice
Heydays Pickled Veg (page 208), for garnish

1. Pour out a small pile of Old Bay Seasoning in a saucer. Circle your highball glass rim with the lemon wedge, and dip the glass in the Old Bay until well coated all the way around.

2. Fill the rimmed glass with ice. Dress the ice with the Worcestershire sauce, lemon juice, hot sauce, horseradish, salt, and pepper. Add your vodka (or spirit of choice). Top with the tomato juice, and then give it a good stir to evenly incorporate all of the ingredients.

3. Garnish with pickled veg, a lime wedge, and the lemon wedge you used to prep your rim. May this classic beverage cure what ails you.

Caesar

This Canadian take on the Bloody Mary was created at the Calgary Inn and was inspired by Pasta alle Vongole (page 177). We support anyone who mixes tomatoes and clams. Caesars traditionally have a celery salt rim, so that's what we've included here, but you can change it up for Old Bay Seasoning to give it a little extra kick.

MAKES 1 COCKTAIL

Celery salt, for rim
Lemon and lime wedges, for rim and garnish
3 dashes of Worcestershire sauce
1 tsp (5 mL) fresh lime juice
1 dash of hot sauce
Pinch of sea salt
Pinch of freshly ground black pepper
2 oz (60 mL) vodka
6 oz (180 mL) Clamato juice
Heydays Pickled Veg (page 208) or celery stalk, for garnish

1 Pour out a small pile of celery salt in a saucer. Circle your highball glass rim with the lemon wedge, and then dip the glass in the celery salt until well coated all the way around.

2 Fill the glass with ice. Dress the ice with the Worcestershire sauce, lime juice, hot sauce, salt, and pepper. Add your vodka. Top with Clamato juice, and give it a good stir to evenly incorporate all of the ingredients.

3 Garnish with the pickled veg or celery stalk and lemon and lime wedges. This will sort you right out, eh?

Seafood Platter

At Heydays, we eschew the opulence of a seafood tower in favour of a large platter filled to the brim with shaved ice. If you love seafood, an ice shaver might be a kitchen accoutrement that could add a lot of fun to your entertaining. There are manual ones that take a little bit of elbow grease to operate (but also double as snow-cone makers) or electric options like ours (one of the hardest-working pieces of equipment in our kitchen, but don't tell our range we said that).

Our Seafood Platter includes fresh oysters served with cocktail sauce, our Classic Mignonette (page 39), shaved horseradish, and hot sauce, alongside our Chilled Lobster Salad (page 41) with our Lemon Vinaigrette (page 43) and our Aromatic Poached Shrimp Cocktail (page 46). You can add the Smoked Fish Dip (page 61) or anything else you find at your local fishmonger's! Seafood on shaved ice is a party by itself.

SEAFOOD PLATTER

Oysters

Don't believe anyone who tells you that you should only eat oysters in months that end with "r." That's a rule that pre-dates the advent of refrigerated shipping. Oysters shipped and stored properly will be delicious any time of year. Some oysters get a bit fattier and sweeter in the winter months, when they've bulked up to survive the cold winter ocean, but because we use oysters from Eastern Canada, ours tend to have that going for them year-round.

The oyster should be alive until the moment it is served. This means that they need some air while they're being transported and stored in the refrigerator (that's why they get packed in crates that have some openings). It's usually easy to tell if an oyster has "died" with a quick sniff—a bad oyster has a funk that will announce itself loudly; a good oyster should just smell a little like the sea. They should have some sea water inside the shell when you open them (called the "liquor"), and the meat of the oyster should look plump and glossy rather than dried up.

Before we opened in 2020, there wasn't anywhere in Sauble Beach that served oysters. Adding them to our menu felt like a classic choice but also helped us stay in a beachy frame of mind. Oysters can sometimes feel precious, and good ones can certainly be expensive, but they also feel like a celebration, which is important to us on the Heydays patio. We're here to celebrate the best moments of summer with our friends and family. Oysters are a must.

One of the many places we worked before opening Heydays was a country club on an island off the coast of Connecticut. This place influenced us in many ways, but it certainly informed our views on this humble mollusc. We would serve them with mignonette on fancy plates in the club's dining room one night, and the next night we'd be standing in front of a plastic folding table eating those same oysters out of our hands, passing lemon halves around for a squeeze.

One of our favourite moments is introducing our staff members to their first oysters. We encourage them to try the Classic Mignonette (page 39) and the Cocktail Sauce (page 38), but then to simply eat the oyster on its own, perfumed by its own liquor. Sauces can totally overpower the subtle sweet flavours of oysters.

Oysters can be an intimidating thing to serve at home, but buying unshucked oysters is likely the most cost-effective way of enjoying them, and they never fail to impress. We love serving oysters in winter, when you can scoop snow off the ground to pack the tray. In the summer, when we don't have access to our ice shaver, we just crush ice in the bag as much as possible. Keeping the oysters cold while you're shucking is important, and having ice crushed finely enough to cradle the oyster and preserve the liquor is key.

While people have managed to open oysters with everything from a butter knife to a flathead screwdriver, a good oyster knife makes the job much easier. We fell in love with the Toadfish oyster knife, which has an ergonomic grip that gives you a lot of control. When you're starting out, it's a good idea to use a towel or cut-proof glove to protect your steadying hand. It's almost inevitable that you will slip, so go slowly and be careful!

Getting an oyster open requires less of a digging than a twisting. You start by figuring out which side is the top and which is the bottom. Oyster shapes vary depending on their origin, but the top will generally be flatter, which allows the bottom shell to hold the oyster nicely. Find where the top and bottom shells join at the pointy end of the oyster—that's usually a nice place to fit your shucking knife firmly. Applying consistent, steady pressure at this point, you then twist your knife slowly until the top shell begins to hinge open with a little pop. Once there is some space between top and bottom, you will want to give your knife a wipe to clean it of any small shell pieces and then use the blade to slice along the top of the oyster. A muscle joins the oyster meat to the top and bottom shells, and it's very important to disconnect both as cleanly as possible.

When the top shell has been disconnected and removed, you then give the oyster an inspection and a sniff, being careful to retain the liquor as you do. If it looks and smells good, proceed with disconnecting the bottom connector. We do this by making a little scooping motion away from us, keeping our shucker as close to the curve of the shell as possible. Then we take a look and make sure there are no bits of shell left inside, removing any with the point of our shucker. Sometimes the hinge integrity isn't so great, and it leaves little pieces of shell inside. Occasionally, you'll also see some shell-like pieces at the wider end of the oyster; they almost look like they're attached but in fact slide off easily with a flick of the shucker.

While we're shucking at the restaurant, we usually place the oysters on a clean cloth until we're ready to plate them so the shaved ice doesn't melt in the process. Once your oysters are clean and ready to go, you can position them on the ice, along with an oyster lemon (page 43), a ramekin each of Classic Mignonette (page 39) and Cocktail Sauce (page 38), and an oyster top shell piled high with fresh horseradish.

Cocktail Sauce

There's no need to mess with a classic. The more basic your horseradish brand, the better.

MAKES ABOUT ½ CUP (125 ML), ENOUGH FOR A PARTY-SIZED SEAFOOD PLATTER AND A SHRIMP COCKTAIL

¼ cup (60 mL) ketchup
¼ cup (60 mL) prepared horseradish (from a jar, not fancy)
1 tsp (5 mL) Worcestershire sauce (preferably Lea & Perrins)

1. In a small bowl, stir together the ketchup, horseradish, and Worcestershire. Chill before serving.

SHAVED HORSERADISH

Once shaved, horseradish dries out quickly, which is why we shave it to order just like in our favourite oyster bars. Using a light but effective Y-shaped vegetable peeler, peel down about 1 inch (2.5 cm) of the skin on the horseradish root. Use a fine-toothed grater or kitchen rasp to create a soft pile of horseradish. We serve this on one of our oyster shell tops. We also add it to our Bloody Mary (page 26) to help cure any hangover.

Classic Mignonette

Mignonette sauce is a traditional oyster accompaniment that combines two of our favourite things: shallots and vinegar. Once again, we don't deviate much from the classic recipe here. Hot take: we really prefer not to put cocktail sauce on our oysters and instead use a tiny spoon to add a few drops of this mignonette and then sprinkle the oysters with lemon. Mignonette tends to enhance an oyster's flavour, while cocktail sauce hides it.

MAKES A LITTLE OVER 1 CUP (250 ML), WHICH SHOULD DRESS A LOT OF OYSTERS

¾ cup (175 mL) red wine vinegar
½ cup (125 mL) finely diced shallots (brunoise)
1 tsp (5 mL) freshly ground black pepper

1 In a small bowl, combine the vinegar, shallots, and pepper. Cover and let rest in the fridge (preferably overnight; see Heydays Tip).

Heydays Tip

Mignonette likes to have some time to "think about what it's done" (as Freddy likes to say). We recommend making it a day in advance to let the shallots pickle slightly in the vinegar. Shallots and vinegar soften each other with a little time—few ingredients have such a delightful effect on one another.

Chilled Lobster Salad

While we are in the hot lobster camp when it comes to rolls (page 129), we can certainly appreciate a time and place for a Chilled Lobster Salad. We love serving this salad with lettuce on our seafood platter so that guests can enjoy small lobster bites. The key for letting lobster flavours shine is a light vinaigrette that will enhance rather than mask them, which is usually our grievance with a mayo-based lobster salad.

SERVES 4

⅔ lb (300 g) cooked lobster meat
6 tbsp (90 mL) Lemon Vinaigrette (page 43)
5 sprigs fresh tarragon, leaves only (⅓ oz/10 g)
Pinch of sea salt
Pinch of freshly ground black pepper
12 baby Bibb lettuce leaves or inner green leaf lettuce cups
2 oyster lemons, for garnish (page 43)

1. Using a spatula, combine the lobster, vinaigrette, tarragon, salt, and pepper in a small bowl.

2. Place crushed ice on a plate. Arrange the lettuce cups lovingly on top of the ice. Scoop a heaping tablespoon of lobster salad into each lettuce cup. Garnish with the lemon. Serve immediately.

Lemon Vinaigrette

We riffed on our classic vinaigrette to pull in flavours that complemented our lobster especially well. The acid here ends up being half lemon and half white wine vinegar so that neither flavour is too overpowering, and the horseradish adds that little nod to cocktail sauce. We use this on our Charred Broccoli Caesar (page 85) as a gluten-free and vegan substitute.

MAKES 1½ CUPS (375 ML)

3 tbsp (45 mL) fresh lemon juice
3 tbsp (45 mL) white wine vinegar
1½ tbsp (22 mL) prepared horseradish
½ cup (125 mL) finely diced shallots (brunoise)
¼ cup (60 mL) Dijon mustard
1 tsp (5 mL) sea salt
1 tsp (5 mL) freshly ground black pepper
1 cup (250 mL) vegetable oil

1 In a medium bowl, combine the lemon juice, vinegar, horseradish, shallots, mustard, salt, and pepper. Slowly drizzle in the vegetable oil while whisking to emulsify the mixture.

2 Pour the vinaigrette into a resealable jar and refrigerate. Shake before using. Enjoy for up to 2 weeks.

LEMONS

Lemons are a key ingredient for summer and seafood, and we try to make sure ours look a little refined. To do that, we have a special cut that yields two beautiful "oyster lemons," two "line lemons," and a middle piece that ensures very few seeds and can be used to make fresh lemonade (page 10).

We first cut the "cheeks" from the lemon so we get two nice circular pieces (the oyster lemons), and then we cut off the two smaller rectangular cheeks (the line lemons), until we're left with the central square lemon tower, which we call the "guts." Save and juice the rectangular guts.

Heydays Hot Sauce

We confess that we love our oysters lightly dressed so you can really taste them. That said, hot sauce and oysters are a classic combination. We get asked for Tabasco a lot, but we like to make our own hot sauce, too.

MAKES 2 CUPS (500 ML)

2 cups (500 mL) seeded and roughly chopped hot banana peppers
1 large Spanish onion, roughly chopped
6 cloves of garlic
1 tbsp (15 mL) vegetable oil
1 bunch of fresh basil (3 oz/85 g) or 1 cup (250 mL) loosely packed basil leaves (approx.)
1 cup (250 mL) white vinegar
2 tsp (10 mL) salt

1. Turn your oven broiler to high. Line a baking sheet with aluminum foil.

2. Place the chopped peppers, onion, and whole garlic on the prepared baking sheet. Add the vegetable oil and toss to coat. Spread everything out evenly on the baking sheet. Broil for 5 to 10 minutes, or until the pepper and onion start to blister but not burn—watch this stage!

3. Meanwhile, make yourself an ice bath by filling a large bowl with ice and cold water.

4. Bring a large pot of water to a boil. Add the basil leaves and blanch, or boil, for 30 seconds. Using a slotted spoon, transfer the leaves to your ice bath. (Cooling blanched herbs down right away helps them retain their bright green colour.)

5. Remove the pan from the oven and carefully transfer the roasted veg to a blender. Add the vinegar, salt, and blanched basil. Blend until smooth. (Hold a thick kitchen towel on top of the blender to secure the lid.)

6. Pour the hot sauce into a clean jar and store in the fridge for up to 2 weeks.

Aromatic Poached Shrimp Cocktail

Who doesn't love a shrimp cocktail? We include it in our seafood platter, and we serve it on its own, an order of three over shaved ice with an oyster lemon and our Cocktail Sauce (page 38). We tend to select larger shrimp so it still feels decadent. We're using one of our magic ingredients here: a little bit of baking soda helps your shrimp stay plump and tender. Adding some aromatics to the poach also helps to give them just a little extra *something*.

SERVES 4 TO 6 PEOPLE

12 cups (3 L) water
1 tbsp (15 mL) baking soda (see Heydays Tip)
½ cup (125 mL) chopped yellow or Spanish onions or shallots (use the leftover pieces from making your Classic Mignonette, page 39)
4 dried bay leaves
2 guts of lemons (page 43)
1½ lb (675 g) shell-on shrimp (size 8/12), deveined and thawed
4 cups (1 L) crushed ice
1 oyster lemon (page 43)
¼ cup (60 mL) Cocktail Sauce (page 38)

1. In a large pot, bring the water to a boil, and then add the baking soda. Add the chopped onion, bay leaves, and lemon guts. Stir until the baking soda has fully dissolved. Place the thawed shrimp into the boiling water, and then remove the pot from heat. Leave to poach for 5 minutes.

2. Strain the shrimp and transfer to a flat tray. Let cool to room temperature naturally.

3. Once cool, peel the shrimp. Refrigerate until chilled through, about an hour.

4. Serve the chilled shrimp on a bed of crushed ice with Cocktail Sauce for dipping and an oyster lemon for brightness.

Heydays Tip

Why add the baking soda to the poaching water? The alkalinity of the baking soda changes the texture of the shrimp, making them both more plump and easier to peel.

Starters

Now that you've settled into poolside life with cocktail in hand, you might be getting a little peckish. You've gotten a preview of our menu as dishes zoom by, and you might have even jumped in on a Seafood Platter (page 30) or oyster course, but that's just your pre-starter.

We've developed some delectable seafood starters that would be just as at home at a glamorous seventies cocktail party as they are on our patio. In fact, our Smoked Fish Dip (page 61) was inspired by a recipe Freddy's grandmaman once copied out of a cookbook from that era and then painstakingly wrote out in her elegant cursive for anyone who asked for the recipe.

These dishes pair some kind of seafood with a tang of mayo or cream cheese, making them all highly addictive showstoppers. Fishcakes and rosé also make a perfect little lunch, if we do say so ourselves.

STARTERS

Crudité & Green Goddess Sauce

Okay, a lot of people order French fries when they're poolside, but we certainly didn't want that to be the only option for an afternoon snack. We also wanted to make sure there was another tasty vegan sauce around, other than our Vegan Mayo (page 143). We use our soy milk–based vegan mayo, but in typical Heydays style, we throw in a lot of herbs, including locally foraged mint that seems to grow like a weed around Sauble Beach. This is a great way to showcase seasonal veg with just a bit of pizzazz.

SERVES 4 TO 6

¼ cup (60 mL) coarsely chopped fresh dill fronds
¼ cup (60 mL) coarsely chopped fresh mint
¼ cup (60 mL) coarsely chopped fresh tarragon
¼ cup (60 mL) coarsely chopped fresh parsley
1 tsp (5 mL) lemon zest
1 tbsp (15 mL) fresh lemon juice
1 tbsp (15 mL) olive oil
1 tbsp (15 mL) coarsely chopped capers
¼ tsp (1 mL) sea salt
¼ tsp (1 mL) freshly ground black pepper
1 cup (250 mL) Vegan Mayo (page 143)
2 tbsp (30 mL) finely chopped fresh chives (fin, fin, fin!)

1 Place the chopped herbs, lemon zest and juice, oil, capers, salt, and pepper into a food processor. Pulse until blended. Transfer the mixture to a bowl. Fold in the vegan mayo and chives until fully incorporated.

2 Use as a vegan dip for crudité, falafel, or anything else that needs some refreshing creaminess. Will keep in a resealable container in the refrigerator for up to a week.

Hot-Smoked Salmon Fishcakes

In this recipe, we use hot-smoked fish, which will look more like cooked fish compared to the cold-smoked versions you might be used to seeing on bagels. We buy our salmon from Howell's Fish, a fantastic producer and local legend that smokes their fish on site. You can use hot-smoked trout or whitefish for this recipe, too.

MAKES 8 FISHCAKES

1½ cups (375 mL) smoked fish, crumbled into a fine texture (kindly do not include the skin)
¼ cup (60 mL) finely sliced green onions + extra for garnish
½ cup (125 mL) chopped fresh dill fronds
2 tbsp (30 mL) finely diced shallots (brunoise)
2 tbsp (30 mL) plain panko crumbs
1 large egg, whipped lightly (you may need a second depending on how moist the fish is)
½ cup (125 mL) vegetable oil
Cornichon Tartar Sauce (page 56), for serving

1 Combine the fish, green onions, dill, shallots, panko, oil, and egg in a medium bowl, and stir just until it comes together.

2 Using your hands, form the mixture into balls (about 1.4 oz/40 g each). Slightly flatten each ball into a puck-like cake and place on a parchment-lined baking sheet. Refrigerate for about 2 hours.

3 In a medium saucepan over medium-high heat, heat the vegetable oil. When the oil is shimmering, it's ready to go.

4 Working in batches of four, carefully place the cakes in the oil, laying them down so they fall away from you and don't splatter you with hot oil. Cook until the bottoms are browned, 3 to 5 minutes, and then flip to cook the other side. Once the other side is browned, use a slotted spatula to transfer each cake to a paper towel–lined plate. Salt lightly while hot.

5 Top with our Cornichon Tartar Sauce and garnish with sliced green onions.

Cornichon Tartar Sauce

This recipe makes a good amount of sauce to serve with our Hot-Smoked Salmon Fishcakes (page 54) but it's a classic pairing with any battered-and-fried fish and is especially lovely with our Crispy Skin Trout (page 165). If you quadruple this recipe, you'll have enough to make this in a food processor, which makes chopping a breeze.

MAKES ABOUT 1½ CUPS (375 ML), ENOUGH FOR 8 FISHCAKES

¼ cup (60 mL) finely diced cornichons (brunoise)
1 tbsp (15 mL) cornichon jus (brine) from the jar
¼ cup (60 mL) chopped fresh dill fronds
¼ tsp (1 mL) chopped garlic (1 very small clove)
1 cup (250 mL) mayonnaise
1 tbsp (15 mL) cold water
1 tsp (5 mL) Dijon mustard

1. Combine the cornichons and jus, dill, garlic, mayo, cold water, and Dijon in a small bowl. Mix well. Cover and refrigerate for up to a week.

Sauble Beach

The June Motel is located off the main drag in Sauble Beach, Ontario, a short walk from the beach. The motel rooms are tucked behind the restaurant and the lobby buildings, making a private resort oasis that feels like it could be anywhere in the world. But it's here, on the western edges of the Bruce Peninsula, which, in our biased opinion, is home to the most beautiful sunsets in the world. In Sauble Beach, the sun sets into the waters of Lake Huron, and there are a whole eleven kilometres of white sand beach from which to enjoy it.

The swimming at Sauble Beach is wonderful—there are three separate sandbars as you go farther from shore, but the shallows (before the first sandbar) are perfect for kids. Windy days are an adventure for bodysurfers.

Motel guests spend their days by the pool, down at the beach, or taking a drive to hiking trails in the area. As you drive farther up the peninsula, the water gets ever more crystalline blue until you'd swear you were in the Caribbean. There are national parks that preserve the waterfront property, keeping it a pristine, if busy, destination for hikers.

During our first summer in town, we were worried about getting our food out quickly and making sure no one was waiting too long. When we appeared a little anxious about this as we were adjusting our staffing, some of our early customers assured us: "This is a beach town. We're on a patio with a glass of wine in hand. Relax, we don't have anywhere else to be." While we still don't like to make people wait, that says a lot about why we're so happy to be in this place.

Smoked Fish Dip

Smoked whitefish is a specialty of the Bruce Peninsula, but you can make this dip with pretty much any fish. This recipe is partially inspired by a boule de saumon, or salmon ball, that Freddy's grandmaman took to every party she ever attended. It is important to use hot-smoked fish, as it has the cooked-fish consistency that works well here and the smoky flavour that makes this dip addictive.

SERVES 4

16 oz (454 g) hot-smoked fish (trout, salmon, and whitefish are all great options)
1 cup (250 mL) full-fat (33%) cream cheese
¾ cup (175 mL) mayonnaise
¼ cup (60 mL) full-fat (14%) sour cream
2 tbsp (30 mL) fresh lemon juice
1 tsp (5 mL) sea salt
1 tsp (5 mL) freshly ground black pepper
¼ cup (60 mL) finely diced shallots (shallots must always be chopped by hand; machines destroy them)
2 tbsp (30 mL) chopped fresh chives (see above, hand-cut only)
1 cup (250 mL) finely chopped fresh dill fronds
Crackers or toasted bread, for serving

1. In a food processor, combine the smoked fish, cream cheese, mayo, sour cream, lemon juice, salt, and pepper. Pulse until smooth. Transfer to a medium bowl.
2. Fold shallots, chives, and dill into the fish mixture. Transfer to a small serving bowl, cover, and chill until serving. This can be made 2 or 3 days in advance.
3. Serve with crackers or toasted bread.

SHALLOTS

Shallots have an elegant and gentle onion flavour and are very versatile. We love them in our Sherry Shallot Vinaigrette (page 81), they are an integral part of our Hot Lobster Rolls (page 129), and they're an absolute essential in a Classic Mignonette (page 39).

When you see shallots in a recipe, you will almost always see that it calls for brunoise-cut shallots. That's just a fancy cooking term for "fine dice." With shallots, the finer the dice, the better. Take your time, cut a bunch of them, and then keep them in the fridge to add here and there to dressings, sauces, omelettes—you name it.

Fried Tiger Shrimp

Unlike your average popcorn shrimp, these shrimp are given a very light fry, making them a fun and refreshing appetizer to go with the Lemon Mayo.

SERVES 4

16 shrimp (size 8/12), deveined with tails on
½ cup (125 mL) rice flour
1 tsp (5 mL) baking soda
1 cup (250 mL) vegetable oil
¼ tsp (1 mL) sea salt
Lemon Mayo (recipe follows), for serving

1. Thaw shrimp if frozen. Peel shrimp but try to keep the tail pieces intact—they make great shrimp holders.
2. In a large bowl, toss the shrimp with the rice flour and baking soda. (Baking soda has magical properties when it comes to shrimp—it helps keep them delicious and plump.)
3. In a wide pan with deep sides over medium-high heat, heat the oil to 350°F (180°C). The oil should be about ½ inch/1 cm deep.
4. Once oil is hot, hold the shrimp by the tail you conveniently left on and carefully lay each one into the oil away from you. Cook the shrimp for about 45 seconds. (Be careful not to overcrowd the pan.) Using tongs, flip the shrimp and cook for another 45 seconds, until the flesh is thoroughly pink. Transfer the cooked shrimp to a paper towel–lined plate. Give the shrimp a light sprinkling of salt.

Lemon Mayo

This is a simple trick that gives a little pop of flavour to really anything but is lovely with our Fried Tiger Shrimp. Until we started recipe testing for Heydays, we really underestimated the power of lemon zest. It has a softer flavour than using lemon juice and adds some balance to this dipping sauce.

SERVES 4

½ cup (125 mL) mayonnaise
Zest from 1 lemon
Juice from 1 lemon
1 tsp (5 mL) kosher salt

1. Combine the mayo, lemon zest and juice, and salt in a small bowl, reserving some lemon zest as a garnish. This can be made in advance and keeps in the refrigerator for up to a week.

Salads

The French hors d'œuvre is sometimes used to describe anything that announces what will follow. Our salads follow in that tradition, hinting at flavours to come: the sprouted lentils in our Sprouts & Greens Salad (page 79) are a sneak preview of the wine-braised version accompanying our Crispy Skin Trout (page 165); the shallots in our Sherry Shallot Vinaigrette (page 81) also reappear in the Hot Lobster Rolls (page 129); and the Picked Herb Mix (page 75) starts on our salads and continues right on through our mains.

Our salads are not always the most traditional. When asked to describe the Charred Broccoli Caesar (page 85), we sometimes have a hard time. It's a plate of broccoli and yet one of the most popular dishes on the menu. As usual, we love pulling in some comfort food elements, like cheese and mayo and savoury Heydays Everything Bagel Mix (page 88). In fairness, our burrata dishes aren't really salads at all, but we've kept them in here because we like the idea of salad made mostly of cheese.

SALADS

Burrata with Field Tomatoes

While burrata hails from the Puglia region of Italy, some wonderful North American producers have adopted the traditional method of enclosing stracciatella (the gooey stuff inside burrata) in fresh mozzarella. Burrata is creamy, sweet, rich, and delicious. This rendition with fresh tomatoes is classic Caprese-style and a great way to present local tomatoes during their perfect summer season. Whenever possible, use local and in-season tomatoes. Field tomatoes are lovely, as are beefsteaks or heirlooms. Cut the whole thing with a sprinkle of Maldon Salt and there really is nothing better.

SERVES 4

8 oz (225 g) burrata cheese
2 fresh, in-season tomatoes, cut into 8 wedges
½ tsp (2 mL) kosher salt
2 tsp (10 mL) freshly cracked black pepper
2 tbsp (30 mL) extra virgin olive oil
10 fresh basil leaves
8 slices of fresh baguette, toasted
Maldon Salt, to taste

1. Temper the burrata by taking it out of the fridge 30 minutes to an hour ahead of time.. This ensures that the stracciatella will be peak creamy and flavourful.

2. Carefully cut the burrata in half on your plate (if properly tempered, the stracciatella may ooze out). Tilt the half-spheres back so the stracciatella is facing up. Arrange the tomatoes around the burrata.

3. Sprinkle kosher salt on the stracciatella, and gently mix it into the creamy filling. Drizzle olive oil overtop, and grind some fresh pepper evenly over the cheese and tomatoes. For a little extra texture and flavour, sprinkle some Maldon Salt over the cheese and tomatoes. Tear basil leaves over the plate. Arrange the toasted baguette slices around the plate. Enjoy!

SALT

Salt has the incredible ability to enhance other flavours in a dish. A few different types of salt take residence in our kitchen, and they each have their time and place.

SEA SALT

Sea salt has a sharp saltiness that Freddy calls "delicious but dangerous." The sharpness works well against the fat in our fries but tends to be most effective when you can measure how much you're adding to a dish (or dressing, or sauce), as a little can go a long way. We fill our shakers with a fine ground sea salt, which means there will be more salt flavour in a smaller quantity. It took practice to get the right dusting of sea salt on our fries, but we love the way it coats them evenly without adding too much texture.

KOSHER SALT

Kosher salt has grown increasingly common in kitchens. It doesn't taste as salty as sea salt, so you'll want to use more of it if a recipe calls for sea salt. It's flakier than sea salt, so it's a little easier to grab a pinch when seasoning a steak or a smash burger, and there's less risk of over-salting.

MALDON SALT

True royalty among salts, Maldon's beautiful crystals add a texture and a flavour that are the perfect finish on a number of our dishes, perhaps especially on burrata and perfectly in-season field tomatoes. Maldon Salt is delicious on just about everything (even our Heydays Chocolate Chip Cookies, page 267). It has such a beautifully unique crystal formation, it deserves its culinary fame.

Burrata with Olive Chutney

We play with our burrata "set" all season long, but we love the bold flavours in this one, and it has the benefit of not relying on seasonal vegetables, so it's a great way to dress up burrata in the colder months, too.

SERVES 4

8 oz (225 g) burrata cheese
½ cup (125 mL) Castelvetrano olives
2 tbsp (30 mL) capers, drained and chopped
¼ cup (60 mL) finely chopped fresh parsley leaves
Zest of 1 lemon
2 tbsp (30 mL) + ¼ cup (60 mL) olive oil
¼ cup (60 mL) pine nuts
½ tsp (2 mL) kosher salt
Maldon Salt, to taste
Freshly ground black pepper, to taste
Sliced baguette or sourdough bread

1. Bring burrata out of the fridge 30 minutes before serving to slightly temper the cheese.
2. Smash the olives with the side of a chef's knife to remove the pits. Chop the olives semi-finely. (See Heydays Tip.)
3. Chop the capers semi-finely.
4. In a small mixing bowl, combine the chopped olives, capers, and parsley. Add about one-quarter of the lemon zest to this mixture. Stir in 2 tbsp (30 mL) of the olive oil.
5. Spoon this mixture over the base of your serving plate. Set aside.
6. In a dry frying pan over medium heat, toast the pine nuts until fragrant and lightly golden brown (ideally you want the pine nuts to go onto the cheese when they are still rather warm). Reserve the frying pan for toasting your bread.
7. Cut the burrata ball in half and place on top of the olive mixture. Season the burrata. Mix kosher salt into the stracciatella (the gooey stuff inside the burrata), and then top with Maldon Salt and pepper. Top with the toasted pine nuts.
8. Zest lemon onto each half of the burrata. Drizzle each half with another 2 tbsp (30 mL) of the olive oil. (cont'd)

9 Lightly drizzle both sides of the bread with olive oil. In the reserved frying pan over medium-high heat, quickly toast one side of the bread and then the other. Serve and enjoy!

Heydays Tip

Castelvetrano olives are green olives that have a wonderful flavour. They're not overly salty, and they taste perfectly of olives. They typically come with pits in, so we place them on a cutting board and press down on them with the flat of a chef's knife until they separate into two parts. We then remove the pits. Once we've got about ½ cup (125 mL) of olives, we chop lightly through the pile. Depending on the firmness of the olives, they may not separate super easily, and it can be a bit messy, but these are such a wonderful garnish, and they add a pop of flavour wherever they end up.

Picked Herb Mix

Fresh herbs are a staple at Heydays. We order them by the bushel and then top our dishes generously with them, and sometimes we mix them into sauces or lentils. On occasion, we've even treated this herb mix as its own salad! It's lovely when you mix in a little Lemon Vinaigrette (page 43) and serve atop a fish fillet (see Crispy Skin Trout, page 165). Whenever you see Picked Herb Mix, this is what we mean, but if an herb mix is like a terroir, use the one that feels like home to you. For this dish, try to get bunches that are roughly the same size.

MAKES ABOUT 4 CUPS (1 L)

1 bunch of fresh dill (approx. 3½ oz/100 g)
1 bunch of fresh flat-leaf parsley (approx. 6 oz/170 g)
1 bunch of fresh chives (approx. 2 oz/55 g) (see Heydays Tip)

1. De-stem dill and parsley, leaving only fronds and leaves, respectively (for our Picked Herb Mix, we like dill pieces to be manageable but not chopped).
2. Chop chives slightly larger than usual and stir into the dill and parsley.
3. Store this mix in a plastic container with a folded dry paper towel at the bottom to help absorb moisture, and keep refrigerated. It should last for up for 4 days.

Heydays Tip

Chop the chives into ½-inch (1 cm) long pieces. If they are sliced too small, they will fall to the bottom of the herb mix. When we chop chives on their own we like them to be cut very fine, or "fin, fin, fin," but in this mix they can be longer.

Shaved Veg Salad

One of our favourite kitchen tools is a mandoline. This small kitchen guillotine can be a little intimidating at first, but if you keep your fingers clear, you will find that it is an indispensable tool of refinement. While there are a lot of mandolines with fancy safety guards, we have found that the minimalist Benriner mandoline is the most effective. Use the palm of your hand to push vegetables over the blade in a smooth motion. It makes summer veg so much fun to eat.

SERVES 2 PEOPLE A LOT OF SALAD OR 4 PEOPLE A SIDE SALAD

1 fennel bulb
4 radishes
2 carrots
1 head of frisée lettuce
1 handful of pea shoots
¼ cup (60 mL) Picked Herb Mix (page 75)
¼ cup (60 mL) Sherry Shallot Vinaigrette (page 81)
¼ tsp (1 mL) sea salt
¼ tsp (1 mL) freshly ground black pepper

1. Using a mandoline, cut the fennel and radishes into wafer-thin slices. Transfer to a large bowl.
2. Using a vegetable peeler, clean up the outside of your carrots and then shave them into long ribbons. Place in the bowl.
3. Using a sharp knife, cut off the base of the head of frisée, and roughly chop into bite-size pieces. Place into the bowl. Add the pea shoots, herb mix, vinaigrette, salt, and pepper. Using your hands, toss the salad until the dressing is completely incorporated.
4. Plate in nice big mounds. Enjoy.

Sprouts & Greens Salad

This is a bright, light, green salad that gets a little vegetal *oomph* from sprouted lentils and seeds. You can use store-bought sprouts for this salad, but it's very rewarding to grow your own. The process takes 5 to 6 days. We like a fine chop on the greens here—it's easier to eat than large leaves, and it means that every well-dressed bite has a nice smattering of sprouts and seeds, too.

SERVES 2 PEOPLE A LOT OF SALAD OR 4 PEOPLE A DECENT AMOUNT OF SIDE SALAD

¼ cup (60 mL) raw pepitas
¼ cup (60 mL) raw hemp hearts
¼ cup (60 mL) raw sunflower seeds
2 cups (500 mL) chopped kale (bite-size pieces)
2 cups (500 mL) finely chopped leaf lettuce (think "shrettuce")
1 head of radicchio, finely sliced
2 cups (500 mL) Sprouted Green Lentils (page 80)
¼ cup (60 mL) Picked Herb Mix (page 75)
¼ cup (60 mL) Sherry Shallot Vinaigrette (page 81)

1. Preheat your oven to 350°F (180°C). Line a baking sheet with parchment paper.

2. Spread the pepitas, hemp hearts, and sunflower seeds evenly over the prepared baking sheet and toast for 30 minutes, stirring every 10 minutes to prevent burning. (Sometimes you can purchase toasted versions of these seeds, but toasting them just before serving yields a nicer flavour.) Remove the pan from the oven and let cool.

3. Just before serving, combine the kale, leaf lettuce, radicchio, sprouted lentils, herb mix, and vinaigrette in a large bowl. Toss until combined.

4. Using tongs, portion out your salad. Top each serving with about 3 tbsp (45 mL) of the toasted seed mix.

Sprouted Green Lentils

We love sprouting, and this is a really great way to add a little vegetal flavour and substance to a salad. The lentils taste fresh and delicious, giving a nice little pop to any salad.

MAKES 2 CUPS (500 ML)

1 cup (250 mL) dried green lentils
8 cups (2 L) cold water

1. Combine the lentils and water in any food-safe container and let soak on your countertop for 24 hours.
2. After 24 hours, strain the lentils and put back in the container.
3. Every morning for the next 5 days, fill the container of lentils with fresh, cold water and then strain right after.
4. The sprouts are ready when there are ½-inch (1 cm) long shoots coming out of the lentil.
5. Refrigerate to stop the sprouting process. Sprouts will be great for about 4 days, covered, in the fridge.

THE CLASSIC FRENCH VINAIGRETTE

The classic French vinaigrette forms the base of many of the dressings we make in-house. We get some variety by playing with the vinegars we use and sometimes cutting the acid with lemon. Usually a vinaigrette is about a two-to-one ratio of oil to vinegar. If your acid is lemon, you will want it to be more like four-to-one because, as Freddy says, "lemon is hella powerful" and less is needed. Our vinaigrette skews a little more acidic with the addition of mustard, as mustard itself usually contains an acid of some kind, be it vinegar or wine. Adding mustard to dressings at home offers a simple way to emulsify as well as an extra *je ne sais quoi*. (Hot tip: When we say *je ne sais quoi*, it's almost always mustard.) If you don't have time for the full ride, just add a splash of any vinegar or lemon juice to oil and whisk together with a fork that has been dipped in Dijon mustard.

Sherry Shallot Vinaigrette

In the early days of the COVID pandemic, we were experimenting with a Parmesan-baked oyster mushroom and frisée salad. This is the dressing we used. Sherry vinegar has an umami softness that pairs well with breaded and baked mushrooms, and we knew the shallots would work some mignonette-style magic on the whole thing. Like the Classic Mignonette (page 39), this dressing should be made a few hours in advance to let the shallots pickle.

MAKES 2 CUPS (500 ML) DRESSING

½ cup (125 mL) sherry vinegar
½ cup (125 mL) finely minced shallots
¼ cup (60 mL) Dijon mustard
1 tsp (5 mL) freshly ground black pepper
1 tsp (5 mL) sea salt
1 cup (250 mL) vegetable oil (see Heydays Tip)

1. In a medium bowl, combine the vinegar, shallots, Dijon, pepper, and salt. Slowly drizzle in the vegetable oil while whisking to emulsify the mixture, about 5 minutes.

2. Pour into a resealable jar and refrigerate. Enjoy over the next few weeks.

Heydays Tip

While you might think of olive oil as a kind of neutral oil, it does have a flavour that skews a little more Mediterranean than the French flavours in our kitchen. We use vegetable oil in our dressings to ensure olive oil isn't competing with the more subtle flavours.

How It Began

In the summer of 2019, April and Sarah became the proud owners of a dated motel in Sauble Beach and, somewhat unexpectedly, a rundown restaurant, too. They needed a restaurant partner who could relocate to Sauble Beach the following summer. It seemed like a tall order, so they decided to post on social media.

Emma Baulch happened to see the post on Instagram. Her husband, Evan, had spent his childhood summers in Sauble Beach and had been casually looking for a project to get him back there, including the somewhat questionable exploration of a novelty smokehouse in the area. At Emma's urging, Evan reached out to April and Sarah to propose a consulting arrangement, as he had a full-time job and wouldn't be able to lead day-to-day operations. That was not what they had in mind, so Evan approached his long-time friend Freddy.

This was a fairly common occurrence. Evan had a penchant for finding wild hospitality business opportunities, including rustic resorts, abandoned restaurants, and the aforementioned novelty smokehouse. He'd call up Freddy, and they'd go for a drive to look at a property and then spend the drive home plotting what they would do with the space. Despite a couple of close calls, nothing had come to fruition ... yet.

If Evan could be characterized by "perpetual exuberance," Freddy would be described as "fervently reluctant," and in the summer of 2019, he was recovering from a broken foot to boot. He hobbled onto the patio where they were meeting April and Sarah, not expecting much. But the four of them got along well, and everyone was excited over the prospect of oysters and hot buttered lobster rolls and rosé. As reluctant as Freddy pretended to be, he couldn't stop thinking about the menu.

April and Sarah felt like "the boys" (as they quickly came to be called) understood the guest experience they hoped to create at The June Motel, and as they traded ideas back and forth with Evan and Freddy, it became clear that this was a partnership that could work. In fact, it was a match made in heaven—the restaurant team could focus on the food while April and Sarah worked their magic designing the space and making it both look and feel like a delicious place to be.

Heading into our fifth season, we still love the opportunity to share a bottle of wine on the patio or fireside, enjoying the property before the height of summer, and "quality checking" a couple of seafood platters.

ORDER HERE!
hot lobster roll
#thiscallsforwine

Charred Broccoli Caesar

While we might be best known for our Hot Lobster Rolls (page 129), this is one of our more popular dishes, and certainly the recipe we get asked for the most. It was originally inspired by a broccolini version at a restaurant in Prince Edward County that was popular around the time that The June Motel opened in Picton, Ontario. We couldn't get it out of our heads, so we made our own at-home Caesar dressing, opted for broccoli instead of broccolini, and added a little crunch with Heydays Everything Bagel Mix—what Freddy calls his "bird seed" (page 88).

SERVES 4

1 large head of broccoli
¼ cup (60 mL) Confit Garlic Oil (page 162), or use vegetable oil
1 tsp (5 mL) kosher salt
1 tsp (5 mL) freshly ground black pepper
2 to 4 tbsp (30 to 60 mL) water
1 cup (250 mL) Heydays Caesar Dressing (page 87)
¼ cup (60 mL) Heydays Everything Bagel Mix (page 88)
¾ cup (175 mL) freshly grated Parmesan cheese (see Heydays Tip)
6 line lemons (page 43)

1 Using a sharp knife, cut the broccoli in half. Lay the halves cut-side down on the cutting board, and then make about six pie-like slices so that you are left with long florets that have some surface area and will get nice colour while cooking. You might want to make a few more lengthwise cuts so you're left with manageable pieces for eating. Toss the florets in a bowl with the oil, salt, and pepper.

2 Get your cast iron or heavy-bottomed pan very hot over medium-high heat, and then add the broccoli pieces. Cook the broccoli until you get hints of char in the florets. Add a few tablespoons of water to give the broccoli a bit of a steam bath. (This broccoli is also great done on a grill in the summertime.)

3 The broccoli should be nicely charred with some slight crunch left. Once you're happy with the colour of the broccoli, remove it from the heat and lay it out flat on a tray to cool. Ideally, do this about a half hour before serving so that the broccoli is just slightly warm.

4 Just before plating, toss the cooked broccoli in about ½ cup (125 mL) of Heydays Caesar Dressing, adding more until you achieve a sauciness that you like. Using tongs, divide the broccoli between six serving plates or serve together on a large platter. (cont'd)

Top with about 2 tbsp (30 ml) Heydays Everything Bagel Mix per serving. Follow with a sprinkling of grated Parmesan overtop.

5 Serve with a line lemon on the side, and encourage guests to squeeze it over the broccoli for an extra zing of freshness to cut through the rich dressing.

Heydays Tip

We keep any leftover Parmesan rinds in the freezer until we're ready to make our Parmesan Stock (page 115) for Cauliflower & Parmesan Soup (page 113). We recommend you grate the Parmesan with a fine-toothed grater or the small holes of a box grater.

Heydays Caesar Dressing

This is a bit of an Iron Chef Caesar dressing. When we were first menu planning for the restaurant, we made this version using just those things we had on hand at home, leaving out the traditional anchovies or anchovy paste. We liked it so much on the broccoli that we decided to use it in the restaurant. Our version gets its umami hit from Worcestershire sauce, which is actually a fermented anchovy sauce. (Did you know they just call it Worcester [woo-ster] sauce in England? To think we've been struggling to say it correctly all these years!)

MAKES 4 CUPS (1 L), ENOUGH FOR UP TO 5 CHARRED BROCCOLI CAESARS (PAGE 85)

½ cup (125 mL) finely grated Parmesan cheese
2½ tbsp (37 mL) Dijon mustard
2 tbsp (30 mL) Worcestershire sauce (see Heydays Tip)
1½ tbsp (22 mL) fresh lemon juice
1 tbsp (15 mL) finely grated garlic
1½ tsp (7 mL) freshly ground black pepper
4 cups (1 L) mayonnaise

1 In a large bowl, using a spatula, stir together the Parmesan, Dijon, Worcestershire, lemon juice, garlic, and pepper. Fold in the mayo. Cover and refrigerate for up to a week. Add to everything.

Heydays Tip

Worcestershire sauce contains barley, so it's not gluten-free. To make a gluten-free and vegetarian version of our Charred Broccoli Caesar, substitute our Lemon Vinaigrette (page 43).

Heydays Everything Bagel Mix

(aka Freddy's "Bird Seed")

We set about making our own version of everything bagel mix as a topping. This mix is fantastic on salads, avocado toast, over scrambled eggs, as a topper for hummus or labneh ... We recommend doubling or tripling this recipe to keep a little extra on hand. We also sell it in jars at the restaurant.

MAKES ABOUT 1¾ CUPS (425 ML)

¾ cup (175 mL) raw hemp hearts
¼ cup (60 mL) raw black sesame seeds
¼ cup (60 mL) raw white sesame seeds
½ cup (125 mL) crispy fried shallots (can be found at most Asian grocery stores)

1. Preheat your oven to 350°F (180°C). Line a rimmed baking sheet with parchment paper.
2. In a bowl, combine the hemp hearts, black sesame seeds, and white sesame seeds. Evenly spread the mixture onto the parchment paper.
3. Bake in the hot oven for 15 minutes, and then stir the mixture and bake for another 15 minutes, or until the hemp hearts and white sesame seeds are turning golden and the mixture smells slightly nutty.
4. Remove the pan from the oven and let cool completely, about 30 minutes.
5. Transfer the cooled mixture to a bowl. This is where your parchment paper comes in handy: fold the paper corner to corner and make a tunnel to pour the mixture out into a bowl. Add the crispy shallots and stir to combine. Can be stored at room temperature in a resealable container for up to a week.

Summer Spinach Salad

with Blue Cheese, Pecans & Raspberries

This is a salad for fresh berry season! It's super simple, but the flavours pack a punch. We're featuring raspberries here, but it also works great with sliced strawberries and whatever else is available. When it comes to blue cheese, we often use a Danish blue that can be found in most grocery stores—it crumbles well and isn't too controversial of a flavour. That said, making this with a classic French blue like Saint Agur or Roquefort can take it to a whole other level.

SERVES 2 PEOPLE A LOT OF SALAD OR 4 PEOPLE A SIDE SALAD

4 cups (1 L) loosely packed baby spinach
¼ cup (60 mL) Simple Balsamic Vinaigrette
1 cup (250 mL) fresh raspberries
¼ cup (60 mL) crumbled blue cheese
¼ cup (60 mL) pecans, whole or roughly chopped
Maldon Salt, to taste
Freshly ground black pepper, to taste

1 In a large bowl, toss spinach in Simple Balsamic Vinaigrette. Tong out into bowls. Divide the raspberries, blue cheese, and pecans evenly among the servings. Sprinkle with Maldon Salt and black pepper. Do your darndest to get a bite with all the toppings together.

Simple Balsamic Vinaigrette

Balsamic can be a pretty aggressive flavour, but it has a time and a place. It always pairs beautifully with berries and blue cheese.

MAKES 1⅓ CUPS (325 ML) DRESSING

¼ cup (60 mL) balsamic vinegar
1 tbsp (15 mL) Dijon mustard
¼ tsp (1 mL) sea salt
¼ tsp (1 mL) freshly ground black pepper
1 cup (250 mL) olive oil

1 Combine the balsamic, Dijon, salt, and pepper in a bowl. Add the olive oil in a steady stream while whisking to emulsify. Refrigerate for up to 2 weeks.

Classic Wedge Salad

We keep threatening to put this on the menu, but we haven't yet because it requires a decent amount of vertical assembly, and we're not sure it would survive the trip out to the patio. We have it here because it embodies the exact kind of summer celebration we aim for with our menu at Heydays. We used grape tomatoes for the photo (facing page), but using in-season tomatoes and a fine dice will help ensure there's a little tomato acid doing glorious battle with the creamy dressing flavours in every bite.

SERVES 4 LARGE WEDGES OR 6 CHEEKY WEDGES

1 head of iceberg lettuce
1 cup (250 mL) Heavily Herbed Buttermilk Ranch Dressing (page 93)
1 beefsteak tomato, diced
1 cup (250 mL) crumbled blue cheese (or to taste)
8 slices of cooked bacon, whole or crumbled
4 radishes, cut into thin slices (use a mandoline)
1 green onion, finely sliced, for garnish

1. Trim the base of the iceberg lettuce a bit with a sharp knife. You want to remove the parts of the stem that will be unpleasant to eat but leave just enough to help hold your wedges together.

2. Placing the stem side upright on the cutting board, cut the head of lettuce in half. Then place each half cut-side down, and cut each half into two or three wedges, depending on your number of guests.

3. Arrange each wedge cut-side up on a serving plate. Pour about ¼ cup (60 mL) of dressing over each serving, but add more if needed for coverage—the toppings need something to stick to.

4. Sprinkle each wedge evenly with tomato, blue cheese, bacon and radish slices. Garnish with green onions.

5. Carry slowly to the table, lest your delicious toppings tumble to the floor.

Heavily Herbed Buttermilk Ranch Dressing

This dressing has all of our favourite things. The more dill, the better. Add blue cheese, and you have a Heavily Herbed Blue Cheese Dressing.

MAKES 4 CUPS (1 L)

1 cup (250 mL) buttermilk
1 cup (250 mL) mayonnaise
1 cup (250 mL) full-fat (14%) sour cream (the good stuff)
1 cup (250 mL) finely chopped fresh dill fronds
¼ cup (60 mL) finely diced shallots (brunoise)
3 cloves finely minced garlic
1 tbsp (15 mL) sea salt
1 tbsp (15 mL) freshly cracked black pepper
Zest of 1 lemon
2 tbsp (30 mL) fresh lemon juice
3 dashes of hot sauce

1 Combine the buttermilk, mayo, sour cream, dill, shallots, garlic, salt, pepper, lemon zest and juice, and hot sauce in a bowl. Stir well.

2 Pour over your wedge salad. (Also great as a dip for crudités.) Refrigerate any leftover dressing for up to a week.

Shaved Fennel & Mushroom Salad

with Toasted Thyme & Hearts of Palm

This is our take on the Alice Waters salad. The chef founder of Chez Panisse in Berkeley, California, was famous for combining finely sliced fennel and mushrooms. While we haven't put it on the menu, it felt like a dish that would be at home at Heydays, and Alice is a major inspiration for us.

SERVES 4 TO 6

1 fennel bulb
1 lb (450 g) white button mushrooms
14 oz (398 mL) can of hearts of palm
2 tbsp (30 mL) fresh thyme leaves
1 tbsp (15 mL) olive oil
Zest of 1 lemon
1 tsp (5 mL) kosher salt
1 tsp (5 mL) freshly ground black pepper

1. Cut the fennel in half. Using a mandoline, thinly slice the fennel (⅛ inch/3 mm or wafer thin) and place in a bowl. Do the same with the mushrooms (paper thin). Slice the hearts of palm into little coins the same thickness as the mushrooms.

2. Heat the olive oil in a pan until it shimmers. Add the thyme, and cook until fragrant, about 1 minute.

3. Assemble the salad: Spread out the fennel over the bottom of a large plate. Top with the mushrooms, and then the hearts of palm. Cover with the thyme oil, zest the lemon on top, and sprinkle with salt and pepper to finish. Get a little bit of every ingredient in each bite and enjoy!

Cottage Cheese Salad with Sprouts & Pickled Jalapeño

(aka the "Weird Salad")

If everyone had a weird pandemic flex, home-growing sprouts was one of ours. We got this great combination of sprouting seeds that included broccoli, radish, red clover, and alfalfa. They turned out to have a bit of a kick (radish sprouts are spicy!), and we kept finding new ways to dress them up. We kept adding ingredients like cottage cheese, pickled jalapeños, lemon zest, and toasted pine nuts for a delicious snack. We couldn't help suggesting it to April, Sarah, and Courtney (the June general manager) when we finally did our on-screen menu tasting with them. The verdict? The salad was too weird for the menu. But it's also so tasty that Courtney requested it to be served at her beautiful wedding.

This dish is all about the assembly. Sprouts look gorgeous and are awesome with all these flavours. If you want to dress it up, substitute burrata for the cottage cheese (two boules cut in half for four servings). Or don't and just call it "fresh cheese."

SERVES 4

2 cups (500 mL) full-fat (4%) cottage cheese
¼ cup (60 mL) finely diced pickled jalapeño
½ cup (125 mL) Castelvetrano olives, pitted and coarsely chopped (see Heydays Tip, page 74)
1 cup (250 mL) sprouts, divided
¼ cup (60 mL) toasted pine nuts
½ cup (125 mL) olive oil
Lemon zest, to taste
½ tsp (2 mL) Maldon Salt
½ tsp (2 mL) freshly ground black pepper

1. Divide your cottage cheese evenly between four bowls (we recommend shallow bowls). Top each with a quarter of the finely diced pickled jalapeño and olives. Then top each with an even amount of sprouts. Drizzle olive oil evenly overtop. Sprinkle with toasted pine nuts.

2. Grate lemon zest evenly overtop each. There is nothing wrong with turning these lemons into your oyster lemons and line lemons later (page 43)!

3. Finish with the Maldon Salt and freshly ground black pepper.

Heydays Tip

Toast your pine nuts while you're prepping your other ingredients so the air is filled with the nutty scent! We dry-fry ours in a heavy-bottomed frying pan over medium-high heat. Just stay nearby to give them the occasional shake—it should take only a few minutes.

Soups & Stocks

You may be wondering, "If Heydays is a celebration of summer, what are soups doing in here?" Well, let us paint you a picture: It's a warm summer evening in July, and as the sun is going down, you order a small paper bowl of lobster bisque from a New England dockside lobster shack, and the requisite pack of oyster crackers is plopped on top. See? Soup can be a summer thing.

We like to add a daily soup special to the Heydays menu after Labour Day. Like all good seasonal restaurants, we stay open until the shoulder season. At that time of year, the mornings and evenings tend to be cool, if not downright chilly. We love the endless possibilities afforded by having an open-ended item on the menu. It means we can go to our local vegetable stand, pick out produce that looks good, make a big batch of soup, and serve it until we run out.

We've included a few of our staples here, but with the stocks we've included and the ingredients available to you, the possibilities are endless!

SOUPS & STOCKS

Lobster Bisque

This recipe was tested at one of the first big family gatherings we were able to have after the start of pandemic times. We use cooked rice as a thickener as we purée the bisque. A lot of the choices we make in our lobster dishes centre on how to make the lobster flavour more intense. If you thicken your bisque with rice, it lets more lobster flavour come through than if you thicken it with a roux (a cooked mixture of butter and flour), which tends to add a lot of flavour to gravies but steals a bit too much from lobster stock.

SERVES 8 TO 10

4½ quarts (4.5 L) Lobster Stock (page 116)
6 cups (1.5 L) cooked jasmine rice
2 tbsp (30 mL) sea salt
½ cup (125 mL) heavy (whipping) cream
14 oz (400 g) cooked lobster meat
¼ cup (60 mL) salted butter
2 tbsp (30 mL) finely chopped fresh chives (fin, fin, fin!)

1. In a stockpot, bring lobster stock to a boil.

2. In two rounds, transfer about 3 cups (750 mL) of the lobster stock to a blender. Add half the cooked rice. Blend until smooth. (Hold a thick kitchen towel on top of the blender to secure the lid.) Set aside. Repeat with another 3 cups (750 mL) of stock and the remaining rice. Stir the mixture back into the stockpot, along with the cream and the sea salt.

3. In a medium saucepan, melt butter on medium heat. Add lobster meat and stir until lobster meat is heated through and glossy, about 2 minutes.

4. Divide bisque into 8 large portions and top each portion with lobster meat and chives for garnish. Enjoy!

New England Clam Chowder

There are various schools of thought when it comes to clam chowder. Manhattan clam chowder has tomatoes, while Rhode Island clam chowder has a clear broth. We take a stand here and opt for the creamy version that might be found on a Connecticut dockside. It is imperative to serve this chowder with oyster crackers. In fact, it is said that early versions didn't contain dairy but were in fact thickened with crackers or stale bread—consider the crackers a necessary homage.

You can see our creamy clam chowder at the beginning of this chapter—behind the chapter title—on pages 98–99.

SERVES 8 TO 10

2 tbsp (30 mL) olive oil
2 tbsp (30 mL) salted butter
2 large yellow or Spanish onions, finely diced
8 cloves of garlic, finely diced
½ rib of celery, cut into ½-inch (1 cm) pieces
3 large carrots, cut into ½-inch (1 cm) pieces
3 large russet potatoes or 4 Yukon Gold potatoes, peeled and cut into ½-inch (1 cm) cubes
Bouquet garni of thyme, bound together by twine
2 x 4.8-oz (142 mL) cans of clams in water
4 quarts (4 L) chicken stock
½ cup + 2 tbsp (155 mL) flour (for best results weigh out 3½ oz/100 g; see Heydays Tip)
¾ cup + 2 tbsp (205 mL) salted butter (for best results weigh out 7 oz/200 g)
(cont'd)

1 Place a large pot over medium to medium-low heat. Melt the butter in the oil. Add the onions, and cook gently while stirring to prevent browning (this is called "sweating" the onions and is meant to result in soft and translucent aromatics without browning them). After a minute or so, add the garlic and continue sweating. Add the celery and carrots, and continue to cook for about 5 minutes. Stir in the potatoes. Add the bouquet garni.

2 Open both cans of clams. Strain the clams, reserving their water. Add the clam juice and the chicken stock to the potato mixture. Bring the soup to a boil, and then reduce the heat and simmer for 20 minutes, or until the potatoes are cooked through.

3 Meanwhile, make the roux to thicken the soup. In a small pot over medium heat, melt the butter.

4 Once the butter begins to bubble, add the flour. Stirring constantly, cook the roux for 5 to 7 minutes, or until the flour gives off a nice nutty aroma. Set aside to cool down a bit.

5 Once the soup has simmered for the 20 minutes, slowly and carefully add all of the roux. Stir with a spoon until the roux is (cont'd)

- 2 tbsp (30 mL) kosher salt
- 1 tbsp (15 mL) freshly cracked black pepper
- $1\frac{1}{2}$ cups (375 mL) heavy (whipping) cream
- 2 tbsp (30 mL) Dijon mustard
- $\frac{1}{4}$ cup (60 mL) chopped fresh parsley leaves, for garnish
- Oyster crackers, for serving on the side

incorporated, and then continue to simmer the soup until thickened up to a nice level.

6 Stir in the clams. Season with the salt and pepper. Add the heavy cream and mustard and stir.

7 Serve by the bowlful with a tuft of parsley garnish and oyster crackers on the side.

Heydays Tip

We have found that the easiest way to make a foolproof roux is to use a 2:1 butter-to-flour ratio in weight, as in this case, where we would do 7 oz (200 g) butter to $3\frac{1}{2}$ oz (100 g) flour. Sometimes weights are the most consistent measure to use in a kitchen, and this is one of those times!

Corn Chowder

We end up with a lot of corn cobs after shaving down corn on the cob for the Savoury Sautéed Corn (page 201). These leftover cobs are the perfect base for a Corn Stock (page 119). Add in corn, potatoes, bacon, and just a hint of Old Bay, and you have an awesome corn chowder that will bridge you from summer to fall.

SERVES 8 TO 10

2 tbsp (30 mL) olive oil
2 tbsp (30 mL) salted butter
2 large yellow or Spanish onions, finely diced
8 cloves of garlic, finely diced
Fresh corn kernels from 8 cobs
3 large russet or Yukon Gold potatoes, peeled and cut into ½-inch (1 cm) cubes
Bouquet garni with equal amounts thyme and parsley (each 3 oz/85g), tied with twine
6 quarts (6 L) Corn Stock (page 119)
2 tbsp (30 mL) kosher salt
1 tbsp (15 mL) pepper
½ lb (225 g) cooked bacon, crumbled (see Heydays Tip)
Old Bay for garnish

1 Place a large pot over medium heat. Melt the butter in the oil. Add the onions and cook gently while stirring to prevent browning. Add the garlic and continue sweating for about 5 minutes. Stir in the corn kernels. Add the potato and stir around. Add the bouquet garni.

2 Cook until the onions are translucent, about 10 minutes. Stir in the corn stock. Increase the heat to high and bring the mixture to a boil. Then reduce the heat and simmer for 20 minutes, or until the potatoes are cooked through. Season with the salt and pepper.

3 Reduce the heat to low and transfer half of the soup to a blender Blend until smooth. Return to the pot. Garnish with the cooked bacon. Sprinkle Old Bay on top for a splash more oomph. Refrigerate any leftovers for up to 4 days.

Heydays Tip

We like to cook our bacon on a baking sheet lined with parchment paper in a 350°F (180°C) oven for 20 to 30 minutes, until nicely browned and cooked through.

Mushroom & Thyme Soup

Mushroom and thyme together feel like signature Heydays flavours. We always have these ingredients in our kitchen, and by now, you probably do, too. This soup is for that day when there's a bit of a chill and you say to yourself, "Mushrooms, but make it cozy."

SERVES 8 TO 10

⅓ cup (75 mL) olive oil
2 lbs (900 g) white mushrooms, quartered
½ cup (125 mL) dry white wine
½ cup (125 mL) salted butter
4 cloves of garlic, finely chopped
2 shallots, finely chopped
2 tsp (10 mL) picked fresh thyme
4 quarts (4 L) Chicken Stock or Vegetable Stock (pages 118 and 117)
½ cup (125 mL) heavy (whipping) cream
1 tsp (5 mL) freshly ground black pepper
2 tsp (10 mL) kosher salt

1 Add the olive oil to a large pot and place over medium-high to high heat. Add the mushrooms and cook, stirring regularly, for about 15 minutes, until they take on some colour and have softened. Add the white wine (to deglaze) and stir vigorously, and then reduce the heat to medium. Stir in the butter. Once melted, add the garlic, shallots, and thyme, and cook until the garlic and shallots are translucent, about 10 minutes. Add your stock of choice, and bring to a boil. Reduce the heat and simmer for 20 to 30 minutes. Remove the pot from the heat.

2 Using an immersion blender, purée the soup until smooth. Stir in the cream, and season with the salt and pepper. We love to garnish it with a crispy fried oyster mushroom or a sprig of thyme. Keep any leftovers refrigerated in a resealable container for up to 4 days.

Purée of Butternut Squash

There's a moment at the end of every summer season when a slight chill whips over the motel property and you know that fall has arrived. It's a special time in a resort town—the days get quieter, but every moment is somehow more precious. We love using our local fall produce, so we start putting soups like these on the daily menu. It's a good option to round out the whole autumn experience.

SERVES 8 TO 10

1 large butternut squash, unpeeled, cut into 1- to 2-inch (2.5 to 5 cm) cubes (about 8 cups/2 L)
4 cups (1 L) chopped yellow or Spanish onions
1 whole head of garlic, peeled
5 tbsp (75 mL) olive oil
2 tbsp (30 mL) ground cumin
Salt and pepper, to taste
5 quarts (5 L) Vegetable Stock (page 117)

1. Preheat your oven to 425°F (220°C). Line a roasting pan with parchment paper.
2. In a large bowl, toss the squash, onions, and garlic with the olive oil, cumin, and salt and pepper.
3. Spread the mixture evenly in your roasting pan. Roast in the hot oven for 20 to 25 minutes, until the squash is caramelized and fork-tender.
4. Meanwhile, in a large pot, bring the vegetable stock to a boil. Add the roasted squash and friends. Return the mixture to a boil, and then reduce the heat and simmer for 15 minutes. Remove the pan from the heat.
5. Using a blender and working in batches, blitz the hot liquid along with some pieces of the squash and onions (kindly do not overfill your blender, and do hold the lid shut with a heavy folded kitchen towel to prevent any accidents). Pour each batch through a fine-mesh sieve into a clean pot.
6. Taste the soup and adjust the seasoning with salt and/or pepper. Garnish with fried sage leaves (page 111). Enjoy!

Fried Sage Leaves

When fried, sage leaves soak up the best parts of the butter and become a crispy, delicious accent to just about anything. We even like eating them as a snack.

MAKES 10 CRISPY FRIED SAGE LEAVES

3 tbsp (45 mL) salted butter
10 fresh sage leaves

1 In sauté pan over medium-high heat, bring the butter to a hot foamy bubble. Add the sage leaves and sauté until crispy, 5 to 7 minutes. Transfer the fried leaves to a piece of paper towel to drain. Use same day (these don't really retain their crispiness stored longer than that). They will taste like the bacon of herbs. Delicious.

Cauliflower & Parmesan Soup

This is one of our signature fall soups. The Parmesan flavour comes through loudly if you're doing this right, and it adds a delicious depth to what might otherwise have been a boring old cauliflower purée. As you'll see in our Parmesan Stock recipe (page 115), we love to use ingredients that might otherwise go to waste—in this case, Parmesan rinds. Save up your rinds and then make a big batch of this soup.

SERVES 8 TO 10

4 quarts (4 L) Parmesan Stock (page 115)
1 large head cauliflower, cut into florets
2 large yellow or Spanish onions, quartered
6 cloves of garlic, coarsely chopped
¼ cup (60 mL) olive oil
2 cups (500 mL) potato, peeled and cut into 1-inch (2.5 cm) cubes
2 tbsp (30 mL) kosher salt, divided
2 tbsp (30 mL) freshly ground black pepper, divided
2 tbsp (30 mL) Dijon mustard
Parmesan Crisps (page 114), for garnish

1 Preheat your oven to 400°F (200°C). Line a roasting pan with parchment paper.

2 Put the cauliflower, onions, and garlic in the prepared pan. Add the oil and 1 tbsp (15 mL) each of the salt and pepper. Roast in the hot oven until nicely browned, about 20 minutes.

3 Meanwhile, in a large stockpot, combine the potatoes and cold stock. Bring to a boil, and then reduce the heat to a simmer. Add the roasted vegetables to the stock and simmer until the potatoes and cauliflower are tender, 20 to 30 minutes.

4 Working in small batches, ladle the soup into a blender, being careful not to overfill it, and blend until smooth. (Keep a thick kitchen towel over the top of the blender to secure the lid.)

5 Pour the blitzed soup through a fine-mesh sieve (this gives this soup a lovely velvety texture).

6 Add the Dijon mustard and stir. Stir in the remaining salt and pepper. Have a taste and add a bit more salt if desired. Enjoy!

Parmesan Crisps

This is a fun little trick to add a bit of umami pizzazz to your soup, or just about anything else. Use these crisps to top your Charred Broccoli Caesar (page 85), if you really want to get fancy.

MAKES 8 CRISPS

1. Preheat your oven to 375°F (190°C). Line a baking sheet with parchment paper.
2. Use a fine-tooth grater to grate some good-quality Parmesan into 8 mounds (about ¼ cup/60 mL each) on the prepared baking sheet—be sure to leave a few inches between each mound for expansion.
3. Bake in the hot oven for 10 minutes, or until golden and bubbling. Remove from the oven and let cool on pan.
4. Enjoy as a soup garnish or a salty snack. Can be stored happily in a resealable container on the counter for a week or so.

Parmesan Stock

When you make a lot of Charred Broccoli Caesars (page 85), you end up with a lot of Parmesan rinds. Always save your rinds in a bag in the freezer, but you may even find Parmesan rinds at your local grocery store, too! This stock is the base for our Cauliflower & Parmesan Soup (page 113) but can add richness to any vegetable or potato purée.

MAKES 4 QUARTS (4 L)

2 large ribs of celery, halved
2 large yellow or Spanish onions, halved (leave skin on)
2 large carrots, top and tailed but unpeeled
1 head of garlic, cloves separated and halved
1 tbsp (15 mL) olive oil
4 dried bay leaves
1 tbsp (15 mL) whole black peppercorns
2 cups (500 mL) Parmesan cheese rinds
6 sprigs fresh thyme
5 quarts (5 L) cold water

1 Preheat your oven to 450°F (230°C).

2 Line a baking sheet with aluminum foil. Place the celery, onions, carrots, and garlic on the baking sheet. Drizzle with the olive oil, and toss until well coated.

3 Roast in your hot oven for 30 minutes, until lightly charred but not burned.

4 Once the veggies are roasted, transfer them to your stockpot along with the bay leaves, peppercorns, Parmesan rinds, and thyme. Cover with the water. Bring the mixture to a boil, reduce the heat, and simmer for 2 hours, until stock has been reduced by about one-third and is smelling fragrant.

5 Remove the pot from the heat, and let the stock cool to room temperature. Strain and enjoy!

Lobster Stock

A lobster stock is the base for our Lobster Bisque (page 102) and can be used in our Lobster & Prawn Paella (page 180). You'll have lots of leftover shells if you're making our Hot Lobster Rolls (page 129) and Lobster Mac & Cheese (page 153), but you can freeze the shells to save stock-making for another day.

MAKES 5 QUARTS (5 L)

¼ cup (60 mL) olive oil
Shells of four 1¼ lb (565 g) lobsters
1½ cups (375 mL) dry white wine, divided
6 cups (1.5 L) chopped yellow or Spanish onions
2 cups (500 mL) chopped celery
2 cups (500 mL) chopped carrots
1 head of garlic, halved
½ bunch of fresh thyme (approx. 1 oz/30 g)
1 28 oz (794 mL) can diced tomatoes
6 quarts (6 L) cold water

1. In a stockpot, heat the oil until it shimmers. Add the lobster shells and thrash (Freddy and Evan's term for cooking over high heat while stirring) for 10 minutes. Pour in ½ cup (125 mL) of the white wine and stir.

2. Add the onions, and cook until translucent, about 7 minutes. Then stir in the celery and carrots, followed by the two halves of garlic, the thyme, and the diced tomatoes. Add the water, and bring the mixture to a boil. Reduce the heat and simmer for 3 hours.

3. Remove the pot from the heat, and let the stock cool to room temperature. Strain (there should be about 18 cups/4.25 L remaining). This stock can be used for the Lobster Bisque (page 102).

Vegetable Stock

We substitue vegetable stock for chicken whenever we're trying to keep something vegetarian or when we just think it would go with the flavours of a soup better. You can definitely use this in our Mushroom & Thyme Soup (page 109) or our Purée of Butternut Squash (page 110).

MAKES 5 QUARTS (5 L)

4 large ribs of celery, halved
3 large yellow or Spanish onions, halved (leave skin on)
3 large carrots, top and tailed but unpeeled
3 large leeks, whites only, halved (reserve the greens to sauté and enjoy, but they are bitter in stock)
3 whole tomatoes, cored and halved
2 heads of garlic, cloves separated and halved
2 tbsp (30 mL) olive oil
4 dried bay leaves
1 tbsp (15 mL) whole black peppercorns
1 bunch of fresh flat-leaf parsley (approx. 6 oz/170 g)
6 sprigs fresh thyme
6 quarts (6 L) cold water

1. Preheat your oven to 450°F (230°C).

2. Line a baking sheet with aluminum foil. Place the celery, onions, carrots, leeks, tomatoes, and garlic on the sheet. Drizzle with the olive oil and toss until well coated.

3. Roast in your hot oven for 30 minutes, until the vegetables are lightly charred but not burned.

4. Once veggies are roasted, add them to your stockpot, along with the bay leaves, peppercorns, parsley, and thyme.

5. Cover all the ingredients with the water and bring to a boil. Reduce the heat and simmer for 4 to 6 hours, until the stock has reduced by an inch or two and is smelling fragrant. (There is some flexibility here to work around your day; simmering longer will make a stronger stock, simmering for shorter will be less strong but still delicious.)

6. Remove the pot from the heat, and let the stock cool to room temperature. Strain and enjoy!

Chicken Stock

Because we break down our fried chicken from whole chickens, we tend to have chicken backs and necks in plentiful supply. This stock could be something you make after a big roast chicken meal or if your local butcher has a plentiful supply of backs and necks, which are perfect for making a stock. We love a rich roasted chicken stock. It's a great base for a consommé or any other soup you might want to make.

MAKES 5 QUARTS (5 L)

2 lb (900 g) raw chicken backs and necks
2 large yellow or Spanish onions, halved (leave skin on)
2 large ribs of celery, halved
1 large carrot, top and tailed but unpeeled
3 tbsp (45 mL) vegetable oil
1 head of garlic, cloves separated and halved
4 dried bay leaves
1 tbsp (15 mL) whole black peppercorns
6 sprigs fresh thyme
24 cups (6 L) cold water

1. Preheat your oven to 450°F (230°C). Line two baking sheets with aluminum foil.

2. Place the chicken bones on one of your baking sheets, and the onions, celery, and carrot on the other. Lightly oil the veggies.

3. Place both baking sheets in the hot oven, and roast the bones for 45 minutes to 1 hour, and the veggies for 30 to 40 minutes—you want nicely browned chicken and veggies here!

4. Transfer your roasted chicken and veg to a large stockpot. Add the garlic, bay leaves, peppercorns, and thyme. Cover with the cold water. Bring the mixture to a boil, reduce the heat, and simmer for 2 hours, until reduced by about one-third and smelling fragrant.

5. Remove the pot from the heat, and let the stock cool to room temperature. Strain and enjoy!

Corn Stock

Yes, really! There is great flavour to be pulled out of corn cobs. We shave ours down when we make our Savoury Sautéed Corn (page 201) and are left with a lot of cobs. They make the perfect stock for our Corn Chowder (page 106).

MAKES 5 QUARTS (5 L)

8 corn cobs
2 large yellow or Spanish onions, halved (leave skin on)
2 large carrots
2 large ribs of celery
1 head of garlic
4 dried bay leaves
1 tbsp (15 mL) whole black peppercorns
6 sprigs fresh thyme
6 quarts (6 L) cold water

1 Using a sharp knife, carefully remove the kernels from the cobs (we like to break the cobs in half first to have a more stable surface to slice).

2 Save the kernels for Corn Chowder (page 106) or a lovely sautéed corn side dish. Place the cobs in a large stockpot, along with the onions, carrots, celery, garlic, bay leaves, peppercorns, and thyme. Cover with the water. Bring the mixture to a boil, and then reduce the heat and simmer for 1 hour.

3 Remove the pot from the heat, and let the stock cool to room temperature. Strain and enjoy!

Designing Heydays

The first time we saw the Heydays interior was in the middle of a snowstorm and there were about fifteen (non-functioning) toilets in the dining room. No, this was not an innovative design choice but rather an indication of the kind of motel update that April and Sarah were undertaking. Toilets had to go somewhere, so to the dining room they went. (There were a couple in the kitchen as well.)

The decor was from another era, the floors were carpeted, and there was a dropped ceiling. But the walls were panelled with wood on a cool diagonal, and the bar had brass glass racks and functioning under-counter fridges. While the restaurant hadn't been operational for a few years, we could see how it could be something incredibly special.

Rather than rip everything out, April and Sarah wanted to honour the history of the space and lean into it. They kept the wood-panelled walls but raised the ceilings, tiled the floors, and built in banquette seating stained to match the walls. They added a gorgeous glass block wall to the bar and mirrors to the dining room, to help expand the feel of the space. They topped it all off with some signature mural pieces that added opportunities for Instagrammable moments. The colour palette incorporates sunset blushes and lake-inspired teals, making it the perfect complement to the real Lake Huron sunsets we get to see every evening.

The result is a breezy and retro California feel that lightens up our food. We put some comfort food items on the menu (fried chicken, steaks, mac and cheese), but when you are served these on pink plates in a bright room, you feel a sense of balance.

We learned an important decorating secret from The June team: greenery doesn't have to be real to make you feel transported. And fake palms don't turn brown (the way all fifty of our parking lot patio plants did). Rattan lanterns on the patio continue on inside, making the transition seamless. All of these little details are part of the whole Heydays experience.

Someday
these will
be the good
old days

Betwixt Bread

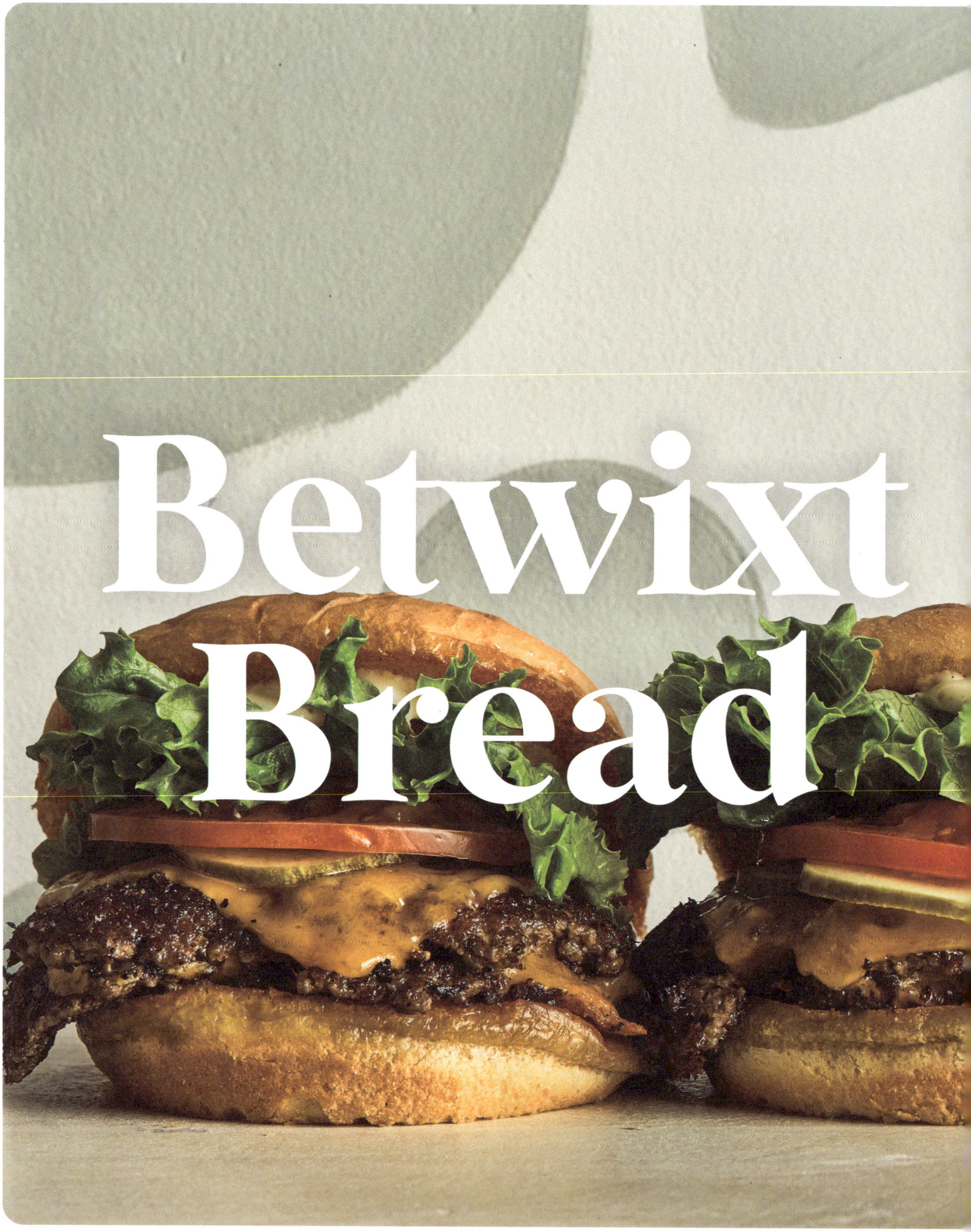

The Hot Lobster Roll (page 129) is the star of the show here, so we couldn't quite name this section of our menu "Sandwiches." It's possible that some rosé was involved with the ultimate decision to print "Betwixt Bread" instead, but here we are.

The Hot Lobster Roll was one of the very first things we proposed to April and Sarah when we met them. It's the kind of dish that can be dressed up or down but always feels like vacation. While we have a lot of burgers in Sauble Beach, our menu wouldn't have been complete without one, so we went with a smash burger (page 133), which we've had great success cooking at home and hope you do, too!

BETWIXT BREAD

Hot Lobster Rolls

Before Heydays was Heydays, we believed the one thing a beach town always needed was a delicious lobster roll. For us, nothing says summer like lemon lobster butter running down your hands as you take a New Englander-size bite. In Connecticut, the lobster rolls are hot. Cape Codders and the odd Mainer might take issue with this and try to convince you that a lobster roll should be served cold, tossed in mayonnaise, but if they did, they'd be sorely and resolutely wrong.

Lobster is meant to be tasted. So we serve it Connecticut-style, sautéed in butter and shallots, on a bun that's been toasted with more butter. Our roll is served with a line lemon (page 43) on the side to give just enough brightness that the whole thing really pops.

MAKES 4 LOBSTER ROLLS

4 top-sliced hotdog buns (or buy unsliced buns and slice yourself)
14 oz (400 g) cooked lobster meat (see Heydays Tip)
1 cup (250 mL) salted butter
1 tbsp (15 mL) finely diced shallots
4 premium pieces of leaf lettuce (see Heydays Tip, page 135)
4 line lemons (page 43)

1 In a shallow pot over medium heat, melt the butter. Add the shallots, and sauté until soft, translucent, and fragrant, about 1 minute. Add the cooked lobster, and sauté for about 2 minutes, until the lobster is heated through.

2 Place a frying pan over medium heat. Butter the outsides of each hot dog bun and toast each side until golden brown, about 2 minutes per side.

3 To assemble, line each bun with your premium piece of lettuce. Using a slotted spoon, to the best of your ability, scoop, strain, and spoon $3\frac{1}{2}$ oz (100 g) of lobster into each cradle of the lettuce-lined buns. Reserve butter and use for Lobster Mac & Cheese (page 153). Garnish with a line lemon. Have napkins at the ready because some lobster dripping is inevitable with this one.

Heydays Tip

We're intentionally skipping over the rather important part of cooking and shelling lobster. You can buy live lobsters and do the whole ride, start to messy finish, but we're here to say there are also some phenomenal ready-to-eat lobster products on the market. Choose your own adventure!

Motel Makeover

When April and Sarah were finally able to share the news with us that the renovation of The June Motel in Sauble Beach was going to be filmed for a TV show, and the restaurant development along with it, they thought the newly anointed Heydays team would be thrilled. We were not. To a pair of seasoned restaurateurs, the idea of filming a restaurant opening felt complicated. We were wary, to say the least, but we chose to focus on the promotional potential.

While it was indeed a hassle at times, the television show also created some fun opportunities. When it came time to taste the first Heydays menu, the show's producer insisted that the food be a surprise for April, Sarah, and Courtney. The only problem was that Heydays had already started operating in its parking lot at a time when there weren't a whole lot of food options in Sauble Beach, so keeping the instantly famous hot buttered lobster roll a secret was pretty much impossible. We did manage to surprise them with some things that weren't featured on the pop-up patio menu, like the Cottage Cheese Salad with Sprouts & Pickled Jalapeño (aka the "Weird Salad," page 96), which we kept safely under wraps in order to capture their unvarnished response on film.

In the end, it worked well for us. By the time we got to our "first" restaurant service on camera, we already had a lot of practice with our parking lot patio and with cooking meals for the film crew. It was definitely an odd time for the crew, navigating COVID restrictions and risk while trying to do their jobs. But it all added to the wild fun of starting a crazy venture together. A restaurant, a motel, an internationally streamed TV show, and a marriage were all born that first summer, reminding us that some beautiful things can happen in the strangest of times.

Heydays Smash Burger

A smash burger is a style of burger where the patty is smashed down on a griddle surface while cooking so the Maillard effect (that's a fancy word for the browning on the outsides of the patty) really comes through. These patties get smashed quite thin, so we don't take a temperature. They're all more or less well done but delicious.

There are several effective professional burger-smashing tools available, but a small sturdy pot will do just fine. We cook these on a griddle, but for home use, a cast iron pan or cast iron griddle on top of a barbecue works well, too.

MAKES 2 DOUBLE PATTY SMASH BURGERS

4 x 3-oz (85 g) portions of medium (80/20) ground beef
4 tsp (20 mL) kosher salt, divided
4 tsp (20 mL) freshly ground black pepper, divided
4 slices of cheddar cheese
2 potato rolls (we prefer Martin's)
2 tbsp (30 mL) salted butter
6 slices of dill pickle
2 slices of tomato
2 leaves of green leaf lettuce
2 tbsp (30 mL) Heydays Dijonnaise (page 135)

1. Using your hands, roll each portion of ground beef into a ball (no need to add anything to it at this stage).

2. Get a cast iron pan screaming hot over high heat. Place 2 of the ground beef balls into the pan with a 6- x 6-inch (15 x 15 cm) piece of parchment paper on top of each burger ball. Smash down the ball with even and continuous pressure (this will require a reasonable amount of force). Once both balls are pressed down to a nice large patty, peel off the parchment paper.

3. Season the topside of each patty with 1 tsp (5 mL) of salt and 1 tsp (5 mL) of pepper.

4. Once the patty is bubbling and the top looks like it's partially cooked, use a sturdy metal spatula to flip it over. Be careful to scrape around the patty before you commit and get under it. Flip each burger, and immediately place a slice of cheese on top of each patty. Cook until the cheese has melted. Stack the patties (we're making double beef burgers) and get ready to repeat the process. Scrape the pan clean with the spatula, and carefully wipe it out with a dry kitchen towel. Let the pan get back to full heat. Repeat the same process for the other 2 patties. (cont'd)

5 Toast the buns. It is imperative that you do your best to keep the hinge of the buns intact. The intact hinge will absorb a good portion of the burger juices while you're eating it and make for a delicious last few bites. Lather the insides of each bun with even amounts of the butter, and then lay them butter-side down into the pan on medium heat. Toast until golden brown.

6 To assemble the burgers, put at least 1½ tsp (7 mL) of Dijonnaise onto each interior face of the buns. In our opinion, order of assembly is critical for best results of flavour and the structural integrity of the burger. On the bottom, place the two stacked patties. Next, arrange three slices of pickle, then one slice of tomato, and finally one piece of beautiful lettuce, with the frilly side facing toward you.

7 Close the lid on the burger and marvel at what you've done.

Heydays Tip

Cooking these burgers can be smoky and hot. A necessary side effect for a deliciously crisp patty! Outdoor cooking is advised.

Heydays Dijonnaise

This may be one of the simplest recipes in this book, but it's probably the one that we are asked about the most. Our guests love the Heydays Smash Burger (page 133), but what adds its *je ne sais quoi* is our Dijonnaise—a classic French sauce that is both refined and simple. On its own, mustard can be sharp, but paired with any fat—in this case mayonnaise and the fat from the burger patties and cheese—it adds a perfect tang.

Dijonnaise is great on burgers, but it's also a wonderful dip for fries and a perfect little side sauce to serve with steak or grilled sausage. We keep it bottled in our fridge at home to use whenever we need it. Grab a condiment squeeze bottle from your local kitchen supply store to keep this and the Heydays Caesar Dressing (page 87) on hand. You won't regret it.

MAKES 2 CUPS (500 ML)

1⅓ cups (325 mL) mayonnaise
⅔ cup (150 mL) Dijon mustard
1 tsp (5 mL) freshly ground black pepper

1 In a small bowl, combine the mayo, Dijon, and pepper. Double this recipe and keep it in a squeeze bottle in the fridge for up to 2 weeks.

Heydays Tip

For our kitchen, we buy lush-looking green leaf lettuce and divide up the pieces carefully for their specific purposes. Lobster roll lettuce pieces are the high-end sportscars of lettuce—the ones that have enough structure to hold the lobster meat and keep the bread from going soggy. The large, flat pieces are perfect for the Heydays Smash Burger (page 133) and the rest gets chopped up for the Sprouts & Greens Salad (page 79).

Heydays

Fried Chicken Sandwich

In the hottest collab of the season, our Old Bay Fried Chicken (page 158) steals our Heydays Smash Burger (page 133) bun and runs off with some shrettuce. Pour some spicy mayo on it and call it a scandal! This sandwich has it all. We should put it on the menu.

This is another recipe that requires frying in a pretty serious amount of oil. It can be dangerous, so you need to keep it together and pay attention. That said: have fun!

Note: You'll need to start this recipe the day before you want to enjoy it.

MAKES 4 SANDWICHES

4 deboned, skin-on chicken thighs
1 tbsp (15 mL) kosher salt
1 tbsp (15 mL) freshly ground black pepper
4 potato rolls (preferably Martin's)
¼ cup (60 mL) salted butter, at room temperature
1 cup (250 mL) buttermilk
1 cup (250 mL) all-purpose flour
3 tbsp (45 mL) rice flour
4 cups (1 L) neutral cooking oil (sunflower oil is great)
12 slices of dill pickle
½ cup (125 mL) mayonnaise
3 tbsp (45 mL) your favourite cayenne pepper hot sauce
½ head of iceberg lettuce finely chopped into shrettuce

1. Season the chicken thighs with salt and pepper. Place in a resealable container in the fridge overnight. In a pinch, this can be done 2–3 hours in advance with a slightly less desirable outcome.

2. In a small bowl, stir together the mayo and hot sauce. Refrigerate until you are ready to form the sandwiches.

3. Set up your breading station: Place the buttermilk in a shallow bowl. Combine the all-purpose flour and rice flour in another shallow bowl. (Note: The rice flour provides that extra crunch that is truly wonderful. Just using all-purpose flour would be sufficient, but the rice flour really gives the sandwich that extra touch of divinity.)

4. Fill a cast iron pan or deep frying pan with about 1 inch (2.5 cm) of oil. Place it over medium heat and bring it up to 250°F (121°C).

5. Submerge the chicken in the buttermilk, and then transfer it to the flour mixture, coating each piece thoroughly. Place on a plate until you're ready to fry all the pieces. Using tongs, carefully place each piece of chicken in the hot oil. Monitor the temperature of the oil and do your best to maintain 250°F (121°C). After 10 minutes, flip the chicken and cook for an additional 10 minutes, or until the (cont'd)

internal temperature of the chicken reaches 175°F (80°C). Transfer the cooked chicken to a paper towel–lined plate.

6 Place a frying pan over medium heat. Spread a nice coating of soft butter on the inside of each bun. Toast the buns cut-side down in the pan until nicely golden brown.

7 Build your sandwich: Spread the spicy mayo on each interior part of the bun. Place the chicken on the base. Then 3 slices of pickles. Then a mittful of shrettuce. Then close the bun lid. This was no small feat to put together. Congratulations! Enjoy.

Summer Sausage Sandwich
with Pickled Veg

File this one under "hiking picnic." We keep entertaining the idea of making hiking picnics for visitors who want to join us in the fall and hike the Bruce Trail. We imagine wrapping up these sandwiches and cold Old Bay Fried Chicken (page 158) in parchment paper tied with butcher's twine, with a steaming thermos of spiked apple cider alongside.

Our summer sausage is a locally made Mennonite variety that has a light fermentation to it. It demands a little acid from pickled veg and belongs on a rustic sourdough.

MAKES 2 SANDWICHES

¼ cup (60 mL) Heydays Pickled Veg (page 208)
¼ cup (60 mL) pitted green olives
1 tsp (5 mL) finely grated garlic
2 tbsp (30 mL) finely chopped fresh chives
4 slices of sourdough
12 thin slices of summer sausage
2 tbsp (30 mL) Heydays Dijonnaise (page 135)
4 slices of aged cheddar
½ head of iceberg lettuce, shredded
2 tbsp (30 mL) olive oil

1. By hand, using a sharp knife, or in a food processor, finely chop the pickled vegetables, olives, and garlic. Add the chopped chives. Stir to combine. Set aside.

2. Heat the olive oil in a frying pan over medium heat. Once hot, toast the bread, getting it nicely golden brown on each side, about 2 minutes per side. You will likely have to divvy up the bread and do 2 slices at a time, in which case split the olive oil for each round of toasting.

3. Spread a nice thin layer of Dijonnaise on the inside of each piece of bread. Arrange 6 slices of summer sausage on each sandwich. Split the pickle mixture on top of the sausage. Place 2 slices of cheese and half of the shredded lettuce on each sandwich. Place the other piece of bread on each sandwich. Cut in half. Enjoy!

Mushroom "TLT"

We wanted to make a delicious vegan lunch item that wasn't a processed imitation meat product. Don't get us wrong, those can be delicious, but this is such a fun sandwich, enjoyed by vegans and non-vegans alike. (For the latter, we allow bacon to be substituted for the tempeh.) If you haven't worked with tempeh before, this could be a fun excuse to try it. Tempeh is a fermented soy product that has a bit more texture than tofu. It loves to absorb flavours from a marinade, and this recipe is one way to do just that.

MAKES 2 SANDWICHES

¼ cup (60 mL) vegetable oil + more for toasting bread
½ tsp (2 mL) smoked paprika
½ tsp (2 mL) sea salt
6 slices tempeh
4 slices good-quality bread (a hearty sourdough is a great choice)
1 ripe field tomato, cut into 6 thin slices
4 pieces premium green leaf lettuce (see Heydays Tip, page 135)
Squeeze bottle of Vegan Mayo (page 143)
6 tbsp (90 mL) Marinated Mushrooms (page 142)
Freshly ground black pepper, to taste

1. In a small bowl, stir together the oil, paprika, and salt. Toss the tempeh in this mixture until well coated, and then transfer it to a resealable container and store in the fridge overnight.

2. In a sauté pan over medium-high heat, fry the tempeh until crispy on each side, 8 to 10 minutes.

3. Brush both sides of your bread with a little vegetable oil, and then toast in a pan over medium-high heat, about 3 minutes per side.

4. Cover the inside of each piece of toasted bread with a liberal amount of vegan mayo. Assemble your sandwich in this order: green leaf lettuce (on both sides of bread), tomato slices, 3 tbsp (45 mL) Marinated Mushrooms, and 3 pieces of crisp-fried tempeh. Dust the fried tempeh with a couple cranks of fresh pepper. Top with the other slice of bread and, baby, you got a sandwich! Excellent choice!

Marinated Mushrooms

Made to be a topper for our Mushroom "TLT" (page 141), these are also wonderful on top of a Heydays Smash Burger (page 133) and are fun to have on hand.

MAKES ENOUGH FOR 2 TO 4 SANDWICHES

16 cups (4 L) water
2 tsp (10 mL) kosher salt + 2 tbsp (30 mL) for salting the boiling water
16 oz (454 g) portobello mushrooms, cut into ¼-inch (5 mm) slices
½ cup (125 mL) Classic Mignonette (page 39)
¼ cup (60 mL) olive oil
2 tbsp (30 mL) finely chopped fresh flat-leaf parsley
2 tsp (10 mL) brown sugar
1 tsp (5 mL) dried oregano
1 tsp (5 mL) freshly ground black pepper
2 cloves of garlic, finely grated (about 2 tsp/10 mL)
4 dried bay leaves

1. In a medium pot, bring the water and 2 tbsp (30 mL) of the kosher salt to a boil. Once boiling, give the mushrooms a little blanching bath in the water for about 1½ minutes. Strain the mushrooms and let cool for a few moments.

2. In the meantime, in a steel mixing bowl, combine the mignonette, oil, parsley, brown sugar, oregano, pepper, garlic, and bay leaves.

3. Add the strained mushrooms and gently stir to combine.

4. Transfer the mixture to a resealable container and marinate in the fridge overnight before using. These will keep in the refrigerator for up to 2 weeks.

Vegan Mayo

We use this mayo on our Mushroom "TLT" (page 141), and it's always used as a dip for fries by anyone who doesn't want regular mayo. We had encountered some delicious soy milk–based mayos before and loved them, so we thought it would be a nice add-on to the Heydays menu.

One of our favourite ways to incorporate garlic is to grate cloves on a kitchen rasp. The end result is like a garlic paste that can be easily added into sauces and will ensure you don't get unwanted chunks.

MAKES 3¼ CUPS (810 ML)

1 cup (250 mL) unsweetened plain soy milk
2 tbsp (30 mL) Dijon mustard
1 tsp (5 mL) grated lemon zest
1 tbsp (15 mL) fresh lemon juice
1½ tsp (7 mL) sea salt
2 cloves of garlic, finely grated
2 cups (500 mL) vegetable oil

1 In a blender, combine the soy milk, Dijon, lemon zest and juice, salt, and grated garlic.

2 Starting the blender on low speed, slowly drizzle in the oil, increasing the power of the blender to medium or medium-high once you have added 80% of the oil. Blend until the mixture has emulsified to a mayonnaise consistency. Transfer to a resealable container and refrigerate for up to a week.

Macerated Onions

We love these macerated onions as an elevated condiment for sausages and hot dogs, vegan or otherwise! For a while we were serving them on our vegan bratwurst, but they really can go on anything and are good to have on hand. The mustard really helps to almost pickle and soften the onion flavour over time.

MAKES ABOUT 2½ CUPS (625 ML)

2 cups (500 mL) finely sliced Spanish onions (use a mandoline)
½ cup (125 mL) grainy mustard
½ tsp (2 mL) kosher salt

1 Combine the sliced onions, mustard, and salt in a bowl. Cover and let marinate in the fridge for a few hours before serving.

Big & Savoury

Heydays

It's been a perfect day so far, hasn't it? The hot sun has sunk below the horizon and the light breeze feels nice on skin that's still a little warm from the day at the beach. This section of our menu is by no means light fare, but it might be just what you're craving after a whole day of swimming and building sandcastles.

We tried to think of all of our favourite classic dishes that feel like a celebration on a plate, and this is where we landed. The best way to go is to order one of each for the table and have a little bit of everything. You've probably already cooked everything in this section before, but we worked hard to make each dish the best possible version we've ever eaten, so we're sharing what we learned.

BIG & SAVOURY

Classic Mac & Cheese

This dish made it onto the menu because one of our past businesses was a mac and cheese shop in Toronto's west end, and we knew how much people love to dig into a big bowl in the summertime. It may be a little counterintuitive because it's certainly a rich dish, but it just feels like it should be served at a poolside barbecue. Ours is a pretty big portion, so we love it when a table splits an order to enjoy alongside Old Bay Fried Chicken (page 158) or Hot Lobster Rolls (page 129).

SERVES 2 TO 4

32 cups (8 L) water
2 tbsp (30 mL) kosher salt
16 oz (454 g) package desired dried pasta (you will need to end up with 4 cups/1 L cooked pasta)
2 tbsp (30 mL) olive oil
10 oz (284 g) Béchamel Sauce (page 154)
3 oz (85 g) shredded cheese mix (pre-mixed or combine mozzarella, Parmesan, gouda, and provolone; see Heydays Tip, page 153)
4 slices or 3 oz (85 g) cheddar cheese, for topping

1 Fill a large pot three-quarters full of water and bring to a boil. Stir in the salt. Add the pasta and cook it for only half the time the package directions call for. Set a timer.

2 When the timer is up, strain the pasta. Do not rinse it under water. Transfer the pasta to a large bowl. Add the olive oil, stirring to coat the pasta evenly. Set aside to cool at room temperature. (This step can be done a day or two in advance.) Keep the pasta covered in the refrigerator once it has cooled down.

3 When you are ready to bake your pasta, preheat your oven to 450°F (230°C).

4 In a pot or deep-rimmed frying pan over medium heat, begin heating the béchamel, stirring frequently. Add the shredded mixed cheese blend. Stir. Once the cheese has started to melt, add the cooled pasta and stir until the sauce and cheese are incorporated into the pasta.

5 Using a rubber spatula, scoop the pasta mixture into an oven-proof baking dish. Lay the slices of cheddar cheese on top of the mac, covering the maximum surface area.

6 Place the dish into the hot oven and bake for 10 minutes, until the top layer of cheese is bubbly and slightly browned. Enjoy!

Lobster Mac & Cheese

This recipe is really just our Classic Mac but with lobster shallot butter, leftover from cooking our Hot Lobster Rolls (page 129), and a whole portion of lobster stirred in. It is the most delightfully decadent thing we have on the menu, and like the Lobster Bisque (page 102), it will always remind us of Lobster Fiasco Christmas in Connecticut.

SERVES 2 TO 4

¼ cup (60 mL) butter
1 tbsp (15 mL) finely diced shallots
10 oz (280 g) cooked lobster meat
10 oz (280 g) Béchamel Sauce (page 154)
3 oz (85 g) shredded cheese mix (pre-mixed or combine mozzarella, Parmesan, gouda, and provolone; see Heydays Tip)
4 cups (1 L) cooked cavatappi pasta (see Classic Mac & Cheese on page 151)
4 slices or 3 oz (85 g) cheddar cheese, for topping

1. Preheat your oven to 450°F (230°C).

2. In a pot or deep frying pan over medium heat, melt the butter. Add the shallots, and cook gently while stirring to prevent browning (this is called "sweating"), about 1 minute. Add the lobster, and cook for about 2 minutes, until the shallot butter mixture starts to take on a lobster hue. Add the béchamel and shredded cheese, and cook, stirring often, until the cheese starts to melt. Then add the cooked pasta and stir until the sauce and cheese are incorporated into the pasta.

3. Using a rubber spatula, scoop the pasta mixture into an ovenproof baking dish. Lay the slices of cheddar cheese on top of the mac, covering the maximum surface area.

4. Place the mac into the hot oven and bake for 10 minutes, until the top layer of cheese is bubbly and slightly browned. (You might want to put a baking sheet under the mac to prevent the sauce from bubbling up over the sides of your baking dish and into the bottom of your oven.)

Heydays Tip

If you can't find a shredded cheese mix that includes mozzarella, Parmesan, gouda, and provolone, throwing a 0.35 oz (10 g) cube of each into a food processor fitted with the shredding attachment is a great way to go.

Béchamel Sauce

We might have a thing for classic French sauces, but béchamel is, by far, the most useful. This is what makes an incredible mac and cheese, and could also be the base of a great soup. A little Dijon mustard in ours adds that *je ne sais quoi*, but otherwise, it's entirely traditional.

Makes enough béchamel sauce for a batch of both Classic Mac (page 151) and our Lobster Mac & Cheese (page 153).

1 cup (250 mL) salted butter
1 cup (250 mL) chopped yellow or Spanish onions
Cloves from 1 head of garlic
4 sprigs fresh thyme, leaves picked
2 dried bay leaves
2 whole cloves
1 cup (250 mL) all-purpose flour
1 tbsp (15 mL) Dijon mustard
1 tbsp (15 mL) freshly ground black pepper
1 tbsp (15 mL) kosher salt
5½ cups (1.3 L) homogenized (3.25%) milk (1 bag in Canada)

1. In a medium pot over medium heat, melt the butter. Add the aromatics—the onions, garlic cloves, thyme, bay leaves, and whole cloves—and cook until the onions are translucent, 5 to 7 minutes.

2. Meanwhile, in a small pot over low to medium heat, begin warming the milk (ideally it should reach about 150°F/65°C).

3. Once the onions are ready, add the flour, and cook, stirring rather frequently, until it smells nice and nutty, about 5 minutes.

4. Add the warmed milk and continue to cook, stirring continuously, until thickened (it should happen fairly quickly). Stir in the Dijon, salt, and pepper.

5. Remove the pan from the heat and strain the sauce through a cap strainer or fine-mesh sieve.

The Parking Lot Pop-Up

The June Motel in Sauble Beach and Heydays with it were originally supposed to open in May 2020. In late fall of 2019, the burgeoning partnership between the motel and restaurant teams was thriving. There was a project plan and a workback schedule—everything was seemingly on track. By early March 2020, though, news about the coronavirus was reaching a fever pitch, and the word "lockdown" was starting to get tossed around. While we had opened plenty of restaurants before, nothing could have prepared us for opening a restaurant in the middle of a global pandemic. Before we even understood what was happening in the world, it was clear that the motel launch was going to be delayed. But there was a restaurant full of functioning equipment, and we wanted to get started.

At first, the only option permitted due to the COVID-19 pandemic restrictions was to serve takeout, so we planned to do a selection of cottage drop-offs that would hint at the menu to come—seasoned steaks ready to be thrown on the grill, ready-to-bake mac and cheese, oysters packed with ice and a Heydays-branded shucking knife, bottled cocktails and wines not available in the local bottle shop. Emma coined the "Cottage Drop" tagline: "For the lazy, sunburned cottage cooks who love the good things in life."

The rules and regulations changed faster than we could utter our new tagline aloud. Before long, patio dining was allowed again. To top it off, the liquor licence rules had changed so that all you needed was a makeshift barrier to create more outdoor dining space. This was to allow for as much social distancing and air circulation as possible. With renovations on the restaurant ongoing, we decided the front parking lot of Heydays would be the perfect spot for our new patio.

From Monday to Thursday, it was a full-on construction zone inside the restaurant and in the motel, and on weekends our parking lot turned into Sauble's coolest new restaurant. We served crisp bottles of rosé, oysters, and a large part of our menu in takeout containers at picnic tables ... all while filming a television show for Netflix.

The pandemic was incredibly hard on restaurants—cash flow became erratic, many could no longer provide stable employment for their staff, and menus often didn't transition well to takeout. With Heydays, we had the freedom to start from scratch, and our patrons were hungry to give us a try, even if we might have seemed a little strange at first.

Given the unpredictability of the restaurant business at the time, we wanted to keep our staff as small as possible, so we started with a counter service model. People would order their food and drinks at the door (to an unfinished restaurant), sit down at a picnic table, and then food would be brought out to them. Admittedly, it wasn't ideal: wait times were long, and things got a little hairy when the tables were full. But people were incredibly patient, and after a couple of months of lockdown, most were just excited to be eating at a restaurant again.

There was something magical about that parking lot space. On the Friday we were to open, the lot was still filled with the construction crew's trucks and tools. As they cleared out, they were replaced with nine socially distanced picnic tables. For our patio boundary, we built planter structures that housed fifty palm plants all around. In the space of a few hours, the very first iteration of Heydays was born.

What we quickly realized was that it didn't take much to create beautiful memories. "Someday, these will be the good old days" became the new tagline for Heydays at The June Motel. We laughed because at first it seemed ironic, as we were living through a pandemic, but it became truer than ever. It was a reminder to cherish the beautiful moments and the people we love while we have them.

Heydays is about celebration and, more specifically, celebrating unforgettable summer moments with the people you love.

HEYDAYS RESTAURANT
TAKE OUT & POP-UP
OPEN JULY 10
519 270 1319
ACE HILL

Old Bay Fried Chicken

We wanted heavy-hitting classics on our menu, and after a lot of experimenting, this fried chicken made the cut. Our secret (that we're publishing in a cookbook ...) is the ratio of regular flour to rice flour and the Old Bay dry cure that happens the night before. Using Old Bay allows this fried chicken to marry comfort food with some classic seafood accent flavours. The skin stays delectably crispy and might even be better the day after, served at breakfast. Just ask Sarah Sklash—this is one of her favourite dishes, and she happens to be a fried chicken connoisseur.

SERVES 2 TO 4

1 whole chicken (about 3 lb/1.35 kg), cut into 8 pieces (see Heydays Tip)
¼ cup (60 mL) Old Bay Seasoning
2 cups (500 mL) buttermilk
2 cups (500 mL) all-purpose flour
¼ cup (60 mL) rice flour
8 cups (2 L) vegetable oil

1. Liberally season the chicken on every side with the Old Bay. In an ideal A+ world, you would leave this to marinate in a sealed container overnight, in the fridge. In a pinch, 2 to 3 hours of marination is passable but gets a C-.

2. In a deep pot or Dutch oven, heat the oil until it reaches 250°F (120°C).

3. Meanwhile, set up a breading station: Pour the buttermilk into a shallow bowl. In a different shallow bowl, stir together the all-purpose flour and rice flour. Submerge the chicken in the buttermilk. Then dredge the chicken in the flour mixture and place on a tray or plate until you're ready to fry.

4. Once your oil is at temperature, carefully lower the chicken pieces into the pot, making sure not to overcrowd them. (You may want to cook the chicken in two batches.) Fry the chicken for 20 minutes, flipping the pieces about halfway through, until cooked through. White meat should reach a minimum of 160°F (71°C) at the thickest part of the breast using an internal meat thermometer; the temperature will continue to rise slightly as it rests.

5. Using tongs, carefully remove the chicken from the oil, and let the chicken rest on a wire rack or paper towel–lined baking sheet. Season the chicken with a bit more Old Bay. Enjoy!

Heydays Tip

Butcher the chicken into 8 pieces by cutting the breast in half crosswise to get two breast pieces, one with the wing attached. To facilitate a more even cook time, ensure the tapered end of the breast is a little bit bigger than the wing side, where the breast is thicker. Reserve the chicken back for making a stock another day (freezing it works great). For the final cut of the chicken, you should have: 2 x legs, 2 x thighs, 2 x breast tips, 2 x wing-end breasts.

Striploin with Confit Garlic

This is one of motel owner April's favourite items on the menu: a classic steak, done right.

There's nothing like going to a classic steakhouse to celebrate a special event—a birthday, an anniversary, any big achievement. We wanted to capture a little bit of that feeling at Heydays, but then serve it up on a matte pink plate. We work with local Bruce County beef producers and get great-quality steaks, about 1 inch (2.5 cm) thick, and usually recommend cooking them to medium-rare.

MAKES 1 STEAK (SHARE ONLY IF YOU WANT TO)

14 oz (400 g) striploin, 1 inch (2.5 cm) thick
1 tsp (5 mL) kosher salt
1 tsp (5 mL) freshly ground black pepper
1 tbsp (15 mL) vegetable oil
3 tbsp (45 mL) salted butter
4 sprigs fresh thyme
1 head Confit Garlic (page 162)

1 Heat a cast iron or heavy-bottomed pan to medium-high (you'll know it's ready when a drop of water sizzles aggressively).

2 Season the striploin with the salt and pepper—the steak should be well coated in seasoning; we like to make sure we dip the sides in any excess salt and pepper on the plate.

3 Rub the steak with about 1 tbsp (15 mL) of oil (we learned that you don't actually need to oil the pan if you oil the steaks themselves). Sear one side of the steak until you get some browning, about 4 minutes, and then flip and repeat on the other side. Sear the fat cap (the fat layer on striploin) to render some of the fat. Flip the steak back over to the first side, and then add the butter to the pan.

4 Add the thyme and confit garlic to the pan. Using a large spoon, baste the steak by pouring the fragrant butter overtop. Flip the steak and continue basting until the steak approaches an internal temperature of about 128°F (53°C) for medium-rare. Enjoy with confit garlic on the side.

Confit Garlic & Garlic Oil

MAKES 6 CONFIT GARLIC HEADS AND 4 CUPS (1 L) GARLIC OIL

6 whole heads of garlic
4 cups (1 L) olive oil

1 Preheat your oven to 375°F (190°C).

2 Using a sharp knife, trim the tops off each head of garlic (just enough to see into the cloves and have them exposed but held together by the bulb). Save the tops for a vegetable stock.

3 Line the bottom of a medium pot with the garlic heads, and cover with the olive oil. Place over medium-low heat and bring to a simmer. Let simmer until the garlic heads turn golden brown, about 20 minutes.

4 Using tongs, carefully transfer the garlic confit to a resealable container, reserving the garlic oil in a glass jar for cooking up the broccoli in our Charred Broccoli Caesar (page 85).

Heydays Steak Spice

We love to use steak spice on the grill, never the cast iron. Something about fire and these spices make such a different steak experience. Rub the steaks all over with Heydays Steak Spice, and then oil the steaks to make sure they don't stick to the grill.

MAKES 1 CUP (250 ML)

¼ cup (60 mL) sea salt
¼ cup (60 mL) freshly ground black pepper
2 tbsp (30 mL) chili powder
2 tbsp (30 mL) paprika
1 tbsp (15 mL) ground cumin
1 tbsp (15 mL) dried thyme
1 tbsp (15 mL) onion powder
1 tbsp (15 mL) garlic powder

1 Combine the salt, pepper, chili powder, paprika, cumin, thyme, onion powder, and garlic powder in a bowl. Use a whisk to blend well. Store in a resealable container in your spice cupboard for all eternity! Just kidding. You should use your spices within a year of purchase.

Crispy Skin Trout with Fried Capers

The whole point of cooking trout this way is to end up with a delicious crispy skin that we at Heydays like to refer to as the "bacon of the lake." We do our best to encourage reluctant guests to try it. The crispiness of the skin can be a little finicky. If you stack the fillets and they sit for too long, they will steam some of it away.

SERVES 2

4 fillets of trout (about 3.5 oz/100 g each), skin on
2 tsp (10 mL) kosher salt
1 tsp (5 mL) freshly ground black pepper
2 tbsp (30 mL) vegetable oil
2 tbsp (30 mL) salted butter
¼ cup (60 mL) capers, drained
2 Charred Lemons (page 166)

1 Preheat your oven to 450°F (230°C).

2 Pat the trout fillets dry with a paper towel. Season both sides with the salt and pepper.

3 Bring an oven-proof sauté pan and your oil up to medium-high heat. Once the oil is shimmering, carefully use tongs to lay the trout fillets skin side down in the pan. Cook the trout until the bottom edges are browning. Shake the pan lightly to ensure the fish is loose, but do not flip the fish.

4 Add the butter and capers to the pan. Using a large spoon, baste the butter-and-caper mixture overtop of the fish (this helps it cook).

5 Transfer the pan to the hot oven and bake for 5 minutes, until the flesh has turned opaque (we like this cooking method because the interior of the fillet remains a medium cook and doesn't get too dried out). Remove the pan from the oven. We highly recommend you keep a heat-proof cloth on the handle for the remainder of cooking. It's easy to forget it's hot and accidentally grab it, or there's the possibility that someone else will!

6 Place the trout on a bed of White Wine Braised Lentils (page 167), skin side up. Spoon the fried capers and butter overtop and serve with Charred Lemons). Enjoy!

Charred Lemons

We love this as a garnish for our Crispy Skin Trout (page 165), but we see it working for other dishes, too. Definitely anything seafood, but it could also be a fun addition to roast chicken or a sweet-savoury dessert.

MAKES 4 LEMON GARNISHES

4 oyster lemons (page 43)
1 tbsp (15 mL) vegetable oil

1. Place a cast iron or heavy-bottomed pan over medium-high heat and let it get very hot. Pour the oil into the hot pan. Once the oil has come back up to temperature and is shimmering, arrange the four lemon pieces cut side down. Cook until they take on a light charring, about 3 minutes. Using tongs or a spatula, remove lemons from the pan and let them cool before serving as a garnish. Encourage guests to give them a good squeeze overtop their food.

2. These can also be cooked on the barbecue: just toss the lemons lightly in the oil before barbecuing.

Fried Capers

These delicious capers are an incidental by-product of our Crispy Skin Trout recipe (page 165), but we wanted to share how we would make them on their own, because they could be used as a superbly salty, crispy garnish for other things, too. We could see them on top of the Smoked Fish Dip (page 61) or elevating your smoked salmon and bagels.

MAKES ENOUGH FOR 2 TROUT DISHES

2 tbsp (30 mL) vegetable oil
3 tbsp (45 mL) capers, drained

1. In a small sauté pan over medium-high heat, heat the oil until it shimmers. Add the capers and cook until crispy. Using a slotted spoon, transfer your crispy capers to a paper towel–lined plate or directly onto whatever they will be garnishing. These are best used right away, while they still have a perfect crunch.

White Wine Braised Lentils

with Shallots & Garlic

Necessity is the mother of invention, as they say, and we developed these lentils to give our trout something to hold it in place on the plate. We originally used beluga lentils for this dish, but they can be hard to find, so we switched to green. Serve topped with our Crispy Skin Trout (page 165) and Fried Capers (page 166).

SERVES 2 TO 4

2 cups (500 mL) dried green lentils
10 cups (2.5 L) water
2 tbsp (30 mL) Confit Garlic Oil (page 162)
¼ cup (60 mL) finely diced shallots (brunoise)
2 tbsp (30 mL) salted butter
2 tsp (10 mL) sea salt
1 tsp (5 mL) freshly ground black pepper
2 cups (500 mL) dry white wine, divided
1/2 cup Picked Herb Mix (page 75)

1 In a medium pan, combine the lentils and water. Bring to a boil and cook for about 12 minutes (or 2 minutes less than the package directs; they're going to get cooked a little more). Strain into a bowl for immediate use, or they can be chilled and used later.

2 Just before serving, in a large sauté pan over medium heat, heat the garlic oil until it shimmers. Add the shallots and cook until translucent, about 4 minutes (be careful not to brown them). Add the cooked lentils and the butter. Season with the salt and pepper. Stir in the white wine. Let the mixture cook down until most of the liquid is absorbed, about 7 minutes. Stir in the herb mix and check for seasoning, adding more salt or pepper as needed.

Heydays Tip

Crispy Skin Trout is a good recipe to try at least once before cooking for friends, because there's a real risk of the fish sticking to the pan. Consider this our troubleshooting guide. Your fish might be too wet (more patting!), the pan might not be hot enough (be patient bringing it up to temp!), or the pan temp was reduced when the oil was added (this is why we recommend bringing the pan up to temp with oil in it). This is one of the rare instances that we would say to start your oil in the pan from cold and add your trout fillets once the oil is shimmering hot.

Papillote de Poisson

Cooking fish in a parchment paper packet is both very forgiving and beautiful. It's a lot of fun to build your perfect cooking chamber—adding wheels of lemon and fresh herbs—and then just pop it in the oven. Then, with great panache, you cut open the packet at the table to release a burst of steam and beautiful aromas. You can cook a variety of fish this way, and it can be a very healthy way of doing so since the fish is effectively steamed. That said, don't be shy about the Beurre Blanc Sauce (page 170).

SERVES 2

10 oz (284 g) fish fillet of your choice, skin removed
1 lemon, sliced into thin moons
1 tbsp (15 mL) olive oil
Kosher salt and freshly ground black pepper, to taste
2 tbsp (30 mL) salted butter
½ bunch fresh dill, coarsely chopped (approx. 2 oz/55 g)
¼ cup (60 mL) dry white wine

1. Preheat your oven to 400°F (200°C). Fold a 20-inch (51 cm) piece of parchment paper in half, and cut off the corners to make a half circle (so that when unfolded, you end up with a full circle).

2. Place the circle on a clean work surface. Arrange the lemon slices on one-half of the parchment paper circle, just big enough for the fish fillet to lay on top of. Place the fillet onto the lemon rounds, drizzle with olive oil, and season with the salt and pepper.

3. Place a couple of dabs of butter on top of the fish, liberally cover with the dill, pour over your white wine, and begin to carefully seal the parchment.

4. To seal the parchment circle, fold it over the dressed fillet to make a half-moon shape. Starting at one end, make a series of tight folds all along the edge (where the two pieces of paper meet) to the other end. Once the packet is nicely sealed and folded, place it on a baking sheet and pop it into the hot oven for 10 minutes.

5. Remove the pan from the oven, and let the package rest for 5 minutes.

6. Being careful of steam, cut the packet open and serve. You can use the delicious lemony herby winey buttery juices to further baste your fish.

Beurre Blanc Sauce

Learning a classic beurre blanc sauce was a magical cooking experience. We studied Julia Child's chapter on hot butter sauces to prepare and then tweaked a bit (but didn't mess too much with the classic). We love the high-stakes nature of this recipe, with the constant risk of breaking. You will need a wire whisk at the ready and must be prepared to whisk vigorously for the 10 minutes it will take to incorporate your butter. We opted to skip seasoning altogether, but with salted butter the result is perfect.

MAKES 1 CUP (250 ML)

¼ cup (60 mL) white vinegar
¼ cup (60 mL) dry white wine
¼ cup (60 mL) finely diced shallots (brunoise)
1 cup (250 mL) cold salted butter, cut into ½-inch (1 cm) cubes

1. In a small to medium saucepan, combine vinegar, white wine, and shallots. Bring to a simmer over medium heat, and let simmer until it's reduced by half, about 10 minutes.

2. Have a wire whisk at the ready. Add your first cube of butter, and start whisking—you're not going to stop until it's over. Add the next cube once the first is fully melted and incorporated. Take the pan off the heat if it feels like it's getting too hot.

3. Keep adding cubes of butter, one by one, until the last is incorporated, all the while whisking vigorously. The whey of the butter emulsified in this fashion will soon turn the sauce opaque, and you should notice it thickening. It will take 10 to 12 minutes for all the butter to be incorporated.

4. Pour into a sauce boat and keep warm, but not too hot, until serving. This sauce, like a hollandaise, wants to separate, so it should be served promptly and will not keep for later use. Enjoy over fish with a generous topping of dill right away.

Fresh Fettuccine

You don't need anything to make pasta at home: no pasta makers, no rollers, no drying rack. In fact, we dare you to do it without the bells and whistles just to see what happens. Use a wine bottle to roll out pasta sheets until you think they can't get any thinner, and then roll up the flour-dusted sheet and make quick consistent cuts ¼ inch (5 mm) wide. Then unroll and hang the strands over a string you tie up across your kitchen. The fancy tools are wonderful, but this will feel like true victory.

SERVES 4

3½ cups (875 mL) Type 00 pasta flour (all-purpose works just fine too!) + extra for dusting
2½ tbsp (37 mL) olive oil
3 large eggs
5 large egg yolks
Semolina flour, for dusting

1 Put the pasta flour in a mixing bowl. Make a petite well in the centre of the flour.

2 Add the olive oil, whole eggs, and egg yolks to the centre of the well. Using a fork, break up the eggs and begin pulling flour into the centre until it is fully and well incorporated.

3 Dust some pasta flour on a clean work surface. Turn out the dough and knead it until you can make a nice, smooth ball. This can take up to 10 minutes.

4 Wrap your dough ball in plastic wrap and let it rest at room temperature for at least 30 minutes to an hour. (This step can also be done the day before, in which case let the pasta ball rest in the fridge overnight.) Resting the dough like this allows the gluten to develop and is a pretty important step.

5 Once you've rested the dough, unwrap it and cut into 6 equal pieces.

6 Working with one piece at a time, and keeping the rest covered in the meantime, dust the dough with a little bit of pasta flour and, using your hands, press into a somewhat flat sheet. (cont'd)

7. Using a pasta roller, crank the pasta through the biggest setting 6 to 8 times, refolding and laminating the sheet each time. Then pass the dough sheet through each successive setting, decreasing the thickness of the rolled pasta each time, until you get to the second-last setting (the thinnest setting is a tad too thin). Once the sheet is rolled out, dust each side in semolina flour and carefully place on a baking sheet. Repeat this step with the remaining 5 dough balls. You are now ready to switch to the pasta-cutting attachment on the crank (we like to use the thicker fettuccine cutter). Run a sheet of pasta through the fettuccine cutter. Working carefully, dust the strands in semolina flour and then hang them on a drying rack to dry for about 10 minutes. Repeat this for each sheet. (If you want to freeze any of the pasta, this is a good time: Place about one sheet's worth into a resealable container or plastic bag, and transfer to the freezer. You can cook the pasta fresh from frozen with rather lovely results for up to a month.)

8. For immediate use, remove the pasta strands from the drying rack and twirl each small bunch loosely around your fingers to create small pasta nests, ensuring there is a sufficient amount of semolina flour on the nests to prevent sticking.

Lobster Fettuccine

Confession: We had this on our menu as Lobster Linguine. A true pasta savant called us out on the misnomer, for our handmade pasta was most certainly the width of fettuccine, or fettucelle at best! But alas, the alliteration was too good to pass up. So is this pasta. We have friends who drive hours for it when we sneak it back on the menu in the fall. We simply wouldn't be able to keep up with the demand during the summer months, so we save it—a treat for the shoulder-season stalwarts who are with us to the end.

SERVES 4

32 cups (8 L) water
2 tbsp (30 mL) kosher salt
14 oz (400 g) fresh pasta (page 171)
3 tbsp (45 mL) salted butter
2 tbsp (30 mL) finely diced shallots (brunoise)
14 oz (400 g) cooked lobster meat (out of shell)
2 tsp (10 mL) lemon zest, divided
¼ cup (60 mL) fresh tarragon leaves

1 Place a large frying pan over medium heat. Melt the butter in the hot pan and, once it is bubbling, add the shallots. Cook the shallots until they are translucent, about 3 minutes. Add the lobster meat, and reduce the heat to low. Sauté the lobster for 1 minute, or until the butter becomes nicely lobster-coloured.

2 Add your fresh pasta to the boiling salted water. Cook until the pasta floats (fresh pasta usually takes about 3 minutes). Scoop out and reserve about ½ cup (125 mL) of the pasta cooking water before you drain it.

3 Add the strained pasta to the pan with the lobster. Stir gently to incorporate the pasta and the butter (we find this sometimes works best using silicone tongs, which let you fold in the sauce without breaking up the pasta). Add ¼ cup (60 mL) of the reserved pasta water to the pan, and increase the heat to medium. Continue to toss gently until everything is well incorporated.

4 Divide the lobster fettuccine among 4 pasta bowls, with an even amount of lobster on each.

5 Garnish each serving with ½ tsp (2.5 mL) of the lemon zest and 1 tbsp (15 mL) of tarragon. Excellent choice!

Pasta alle Vongole

When Freddy and Katie were working at a country club on Long Island Sound, they found themselves with an excess of fresh cherrystone clams after a season-end party.

They had the next day off from their respective jobs bartending and serving, and decided they wanted to do something delicious with the clams. The island grocery store was closed, so they spent the day foraging ingredients: herbs from the club's garden, a secreted box of pasta traded for a cigarette, and a lemon snatched from the bar. It was the first time they ever cooked together, and it was both good and bad enough that they continue to do so many years later.

This is the pasta alle vongole that started it all.

SERVES 4

32 cups (8 L) water
2 tbsp (30 mL) kosher salt
14 oz (400 g) fresh fettucine pasta (page 171)
1½ tbsp (22 mL) olive oil
2 tbsp (30 mL) finely diced shallots (brunoise)
1½ cloves of garlic, finely minced
¼ tsp (1 mL) chili flakes
¼ cup (60 mL) dry white wine
1 lb (450 g) little neck clams (discard any that do not close when tapped lightly)
2 tbsp (30 mL) roughly chopped fresh flat-leaf parsley
1 tbsp (15 mL) salted butter
1 tsp (5 mL) lemon zest
Salt and freshly ground black pepper, to taste
Fresh parsley leaves, for garnish

1 Whatever you do, start by arguing about these steps vehemently. It makes the pasta taste better and is the true test for any relationship.

2 Fill a large pot with water and bring it to a boil with kosher salt. Freddy says to be careful when salting the water. Less salt will give more control in seasoning at the end. Working with seafood means there will be varying amounts of brine, or salt water, that make their way in from the clams itself, so maybe you want to hold off on salting until the end.

3 Meanwhile, in a large saucepan over medium (Katie) to medium-high heat (Freddy, who is sometimes impatient), heat the oil. It's best if you have a lid that covers this saucepan snugly. Add your shallots and garlic, and cook until translucent, 2 to 3 minutes.

4 Add your fettucine to the large pot of boiling water, and cook until the pasta floats, or about 3 minutes. Reserve some pasta cooking water from the pot, and then strain your pasta.

5 To the saucepan with the shallots mixture, add the strained pasta, chili, white wine, and clams. Using silicone tongs, toss until the (cont'd)

pasta is well coated in your olive oil and aromatic mixture. Keep over medium to medium-low heat. Add a splash of the reserved cooking water, and cover the pan with a lid. Cook for about 3–5 minutes, or until the clams are opening. Clams that don't open have died and should be discarded.

6. Taste your sauce and add salt and pepper as needed. White pepper is traditionally used in seafood dishes, but we tend to prefer the flavour of black pepper (it can be a little strong for the seafood flavours, so a little goes a long way!). Stir in the lemon zest.

7. Using tongs, pick up a good chunk of pasta and spin slightly as you deliver it to the plate. (This works best if you stick out your tongue in concentration.) Be sure to spoon out some extra clams.

8. Top with parsley before serving.

Lobster & Prawn Paella

We don't have paella on the menu, but we served it at a very special dinner while filming the Netflix show. We captured a celebratory dinner for the restaurant and motel partners that happened to fall on Freddy's birthday, so Evan decided to go all out with one of the most over-the-top paellas we've ever seen—and that's saying something for Evan. This one had enough lobster tail and shrimp for everyone, and we were eating it for a very long time after.

SERVES 6 TO 8

5 cups (1.25 L) Lobster Stock (page 116)
Pinch of saffron (to bloom in lobster stock)
7 oz (200 g) high-quality dried chorizo, thinly sliced
2 cups (500 mL) bomba rice
2 cups (500 mL) Sofrito
¼ cup (60 mL) olive oil
2 tsp (10 mL) sea salt
2 tsp (10 mL) freshly ground black pepper
7 oz (200 g) lobster meat
12 shell-on, tail-on shrimp (size 8/12), deveined
1 cup (250 mL) peas (frozen is fine)
1 lemon
½ bunch fresh flat-leaf parsley (approx. 2 oz/55 g)

1 Heat up the lobster stock in a pot next to where you will be cooking the paella. Once the lobster stock is warmed through, add the saffron and allow to steep while you prepare the rest of the paella.

2 In a rondeau (or a paella pan if you have one), add your olive oil and place the pan over medium heat. Add the chorizo, and cook until the fat begins to render and the edges of the chorizo are looking crispy, about 7 minutes. Transfer the crispy chorizo to a plate and set aside.

3 Add the bomba rice to the hot pan, stirring so it becomes coated in the delicious chorizo-infused oil, and cook for a few minutes, until the rice is starting to become translucent. Add the sofrito, and stir until well combined. Season with the salt and pepper.

4 Using a ladle, gradually add the lobster saffron broth to the rice, stirring but not too much. Cook until the liquid has been absorbed into the rice, and then add another ladleful. Incorporating all of the lobster stock should take about 25 minutes. Once the stock has been incorporated, stir in the peas.

5 At this point, do a little taste test to see how your salt levels are doing, and add some more, if needed. (cont'd)

6 Preheat your oven to 350°F (180°C).

7 Arrange the lobster and shrimp on top of the rice, and cover with foil. Cook over low heat for about 20 minutes, and then transfer the pan to the hot oven and bake until some of the liquid has cooked off and the paella is looking firmer, about 30 minutes.

8 Remove the pan from the oven. Finish the paella with a sprinkle of salt, drizzle of olive oil, squeeze of lemon juice, and a generous amount of parsley to cover the top. Equally distribute the seafood to your guests when you serve, and remember to scrape the delicious crispy rice off the bottom of the pan!

Sofrito

Take your time cooking this base sauce, slow and low—it is the heart of a paella and gives it all that depth of flavour.

MAKES 2 CUPS (500 ML)

½ cup (125 mL) olive oil
1 cup (250 mL) finely diced green bell pepper
1 cup (250 mL) finely diced white onion
1 cup (250 mL) finely diced ripe field tomato
2 tbsp (30 mL) minced garlic

1 In a wide-bottomed pot, heat the olive oil. Add the bell pepper, onion, tomato, and garlic. Sauté over low heat until everything is lightly caramelized and really cooked down, about 1 hour, or maybe a touch longer.

2 Sofrito can be made in advance and kept in a resealable container in the fridge for 4 days. It's great to have on hand to enhance soups, sauces, rice dishes—pretty much everything.

Casarecce with Zucchini, Blistered Cherry Tomatoes & Herb Pesto

We're always on the hunt for delicious vegan mains, and this recipe is a great way to enjoy seasonal vegetables and herbs. The real winner here is the Parsley & Toasted Pine Nut Pesto (page 184), which we use as a base for the casarecce pasta, which might otherwise fly all over the plate. Vegan cooking is full of so many tricks to add richness from plant-based ingredients, while we're usually used to simply reaching for the butter or cheese. Here, pine nuts add the extra body that makes everyone crave this pasta.

SERVES 4

32 cups (8 L) water
2 tbsp (30 mL) kosher salt
14 oz (400 g) casarecce dried pasta (or any short-noodle pasta that you desire)
¼ cup (60 mL) olive oil + a little extra just to coat the cooked pasta
2 small zucchini (1 green and 1 yellow, especially great if it's early summer season), cut in half and then in ½-inch (1 cm) slices on a bias
¼ cup (60 mL) diced shallots
16 cherry tomatoes
Salt and pepper, to taste
Parsley & Toasted Pine Nut Pesto (page 184), for serving
⅓ cup (45 g) toasted pine nuts (see Heydays Tip, page 96), for garnish

1. Bring a large pot of salted water to a boil. Add the dried pasta, and cook for 10 minutes, until al dente. Strain the pasta, and pop back into the pot with a little squeeze of oil just to coat it very lightly. Set aside.

2. In a large pan over medium-high heat, heat the olive oil until it shimmers. Add the zucchini, and sauté for 5 minutes, until the white part of the zucchini starts to caramelize. Add the shallots and cherry tomatoes, and continue to sauté until the tomatoes start to blister, another 3 to 5 minutes. Add the cooked pasta, and toss to mix and heat through. Season with salt and pepper (have a taste to make sure your seasoning is on point).

3. When plating the pasta, first scoop 3 tbsp (45 mL) of the parsley pesto onto the dish and swirl to make a circle of pesto. Evenly distribute the pasta and vegetables among the 4 plates, and garnish with a sprinkle of toasted pine nuts for added crunch.

Parsley & Toasted Pine Nut Pesto

MAKES 3 CUPS (750 ML) PESTO

- 2 bunches of fresh flat-leaf parsley (approx. $8\frac{1}{2}$ oz/240 g)
- $\frac{1}{2}$ cup (125 mL) toasted pine nuts
- 2 cloves of garlic
- 2 tbsp (30 mL) fresh lemon juice
- 1 tsp (5 mL) kosher salt
- 1 tsp (5 mL) freshly ground black pepper
- 1 cup (250 mL) olive oil

1. Fill a large bowl with water and ice to make an ice bath.

2. Bring a medium pot of water to a boil. Add the parsley (stems and all) to the water, and blanch for about 30 seconds, just until the parsley turns a bright green. Using tongs, transfer the blanched parsley to your ice bath to cool completely and stop the cooking process. Once chilled, remove the parsley and thoroughly squeeze out all water. Using a sharp knife, finely chop the blanched parsley.

3. In a food processor, combine the parsley, pine nuts, garlic, lemon juice, salt, and pepper. Starting at low speed and steadily increasing to high, gradually blend in the olive oil until the mix is emulsified and the parsley is blended into the pine nuts (it should have a relatively thick consistency that can nicely sit on a plate). Transfer to a resealable container and refrigerate until ready to use. It will keep for up to a week.

Moules Marinières with Grilled Bread

When we put "Daily Fish" on the menu sometime after Labour Day, a whole new world of possibility opens up. We certainly add these as a special whenever we come across good mussels, but they're just perfect on the patio whenever there's a hint of fall in the air. There may be nothing better than dipping your freshly toasted sourdough into hot mussel broth, and it is perfectly acceptable (and encouraged) to drink from the bowl once you've gone through the mussels.

SERVES 2 TO 4

½ cup (125 mL) + 2 tbsp (30 mL) salted butter, divided
1 cup (250 mL) finely chopped onion
2 tbsp (30 mL) finely chopped garlic
2 lb (900 g) mussels, debearded
½ cup (125 mL) dry white wine
½ cup (125 mL) roughly chopped fresh flat-leaf parsley
2 tbsp (30 mL) heavy (whipping) cream
8 slices of baguette

1. In a large pot over medium heat, melt ½ cup of the butter. Add the onion and garlic, and cook until translucent, about 3 to 5 minutes.
2. Add the mussels to the onion mixture, and then the white wine. Cover the pot with the lid.
3. Cook until the mussels have opened, 3 to 5 minutes (discard any mussels that do not open). Reduce the heat to medium-low, and gently stir in the parsley and cream. (This can simmer very lightly while you toast your baguette slices.)
4. Put a non-stick frying pan over medium heat. Using the 2 tbsp (30 mL) of butter, butter both sides of the baguette slices. Toast them in the hot pan until golden brown, about 3 minutes on each side.
5. Divide the mussels between 2 serving bowls, adding a nice amount of broth to each. Place the toasted bread on a plate. Serve with a fork and a spoon. Enjoy!

Sides

One of the best ways to eat at Heydays is to share everything. Most main dishes come on their own, so we recommend adding fries, a "Veg of the Day," crispy mushrooms (see our Thyme-Sautéed Oyster Mushrooms, page 192, for the make-at-home version), and maybe even a Sprouts & Greens Salad (page 79) so it feels like a family-style feast.

This chapter is made up of some of our favourite "Veg of the Day" options, which are usually inspired by whatever is popping up for the season at nearby farms. We are first in line for asparagus in May and can't wait for the good beets, tomatoes, and corn to follow.

We always try to keep these dishes simple and let the produce speak for itself. Here are some ideas to try out.

SIDES

Thyme-Sautéed Oyster Mushrooms

There is a popular item on our menu called Crispy Oyster Mushrooms. We have converted many a mushroom-hater with these mushrooms. It's very simple. We trim 4 cups (1 L) of oyster mushrooms, and then we throw them in the deep-fryer. We salt them like fries, and they come out crispy and delicious. You could do this at home with a small deep-fryer or a pot with some oil, but we also like this sautéed version, which we make for guests who can't have any gluten cross-contamination whatsoever.

SERVES 2 TO 4 AS A NICE LITTLE STEAK ACCOMPANIMENT

2 tbsp (30 mL) olive oil
7 oz (200 g) oyster mushrooms, picked and trimmed
3 sprigs fresh thyme
1 tbsp (15 mL) salted butter
¼ cup (60 mL) finely diced shallots (brunoise)
1 tsp (5 mL) kosher salt
1 tsp (5 mL) freshly ground black pepper

1. In a large pan over medium-high heat, heat the oil until it shimmers. Add the mushrooms, making sure you don't overload the pan. (If you're working with a smaller pan, it might actually be quicker to cook the mushrooms in two batches. The high heat helps evaporate mushroom moisture faster and caramelizes the mushrooms better. If you feel like there's too much moisture, just keep going! It will cook off eventually.) Cook until the mushrooms take on some nice browning, about 10 minutes (but really depends on their moisture content).

2. Add thyme, butter, shallots, salt, and pepper. Cook gently for a few minutes, or just until the thyme leaves start to fall off. Serve alongside or on top of your Striploin with Confit Garlic (page 161).

Heydays Tip

When you're first sautéing mushrooms they tend to release a lot of water and become a little soggy. Don't give up! Keep going! This moisture will eventually cook off and lead to a nice caramelization. Then we always add butter to finish.

Chilled Asparagus Mimosa Salad

Google "mimosa salad" and a layered egg, cheese, and tuna salad will likely appear. We do a riff on that, using chopped and divided hard-boiled eggs that look beautiful. Mimosa salad has been described as "festive," and it's certainly an eye-catching way to dress up just about any ingredient. Chef Tyler Cunningham joined us in our third year and put this salad on the menu to feature local spring asparagus. We love it because it reminds us of Caviar, Blinis & the Fixin's (page 223), but let's be honest, we love just about anything covered in Heydays Dijonnaise (page 135).

Confession: We called it Dijon Aioli when we were explaining this dish tableside, but really it's just the Heydays Dijonnaise that you have come to know and love—and hopefully have stored in your fridge by now.

SERVES 2 TO 4

1 lb (450 g) asparagus
2 hard-boiled eggs, peeled
¼ cup (60 mL) finely diced shallots (brunoise)
2 tbsp (30 mL) finely chopped fresh chives (fin, fin, fin!)
Heydays Dijonnaise (page 135), for serving

1 Prepare an ice bath by filling a large bowl with water and ice. Bring a medium pot filled with salted water to a boil. Add the asparagus to the pot, and cook for 1½ minutes, until the asparagus is bright green. Using tongs, transfer the blanched asparagus to your prepared ice bath to stop the cooking process.

2 Separate the hard-boiled egg whites from the egg yolks. Chop each into a fine crumb. Keep them separate until plating.

3 Spoon Dijonnaise into the base of each plate (if plating individual portions) or a platter. Arrange the chilled asparagus in a nice little bundle on top of the Dijonnaise.

4 Sprinkle an even amount of the shallots on top each portion of asparagus, trying to stay within the middle 50% of the asparagus. Then sprinkle the egg whites on top, followed by the egg yolks (to get a nice colour contrast of the white and yellow of the egg). And finally, sprinkle the chives on top for colour and flavour. Cheers!

Putting Our Spin on a Classic

When we were starting to think about the Heydays menu, we were drawn immediately to happy-making, comfort food classics. It might have been the nostalgic feel of Sauble Beach, the beauty of the renovated motel, or The June brand itself, but we really wanted to lean on classics that everyone would want to eat all the time. The only thing is, there are a lot of burgers in a beach town, so we thought long and hard about how to make ours special (same with our fried chicken, and our steak, and our mac and cheese ...).

It helps to think about the feel of the dining experience you want to create. The food we were drawn to has its own persona—like it was created by a French chef who washed up on the shores of a North American beach town. The flavour profile was a little French, a little coastal. There was butter and lemon and garlic and thyme in our kitchen. So when we looked to update fried chicken, we made sure it had a light crispy skin and was finished with Old Bay as a nod to a coastal seafood boil. Our smash burger is made a little brighter with the addition of a Dijonnaise. And our lobster roll is served with lemon and shallot butter to give it additional dimension.

Once you have your persona, the little tweaks become obvious. Heydays would look quite different if our persona was a cowgirl hitchhiking to LA, for instance. Come to think of it, we might have to try that restaurant one day, too ...

Fried Beans Almondine

There is a summer moment in which green beans are at their best. We put them on our menu as the vegetable of the day because they're just so tasty when they're fried up with almonds. The visual look of a green-and-yellow bean combination is stunning!

SERVES 2 TO 4

3 tbsp (45 mL) olive oil
1 lb (450 g) green and/or yellow beans (a mix of the two is ideal; see Heydays Tip)
1 tsp (5 mL) sea salt
1 tsp (5 mL) freshly ground black pepper
1½ tsp (7 mL) fresh lemon juice
¼ cup (60 mL) toasted slivered almonds

1 Add the olive oil to your cast iron or heavy-bottomed frying pan and get it screaming hot over medium-high heat. Quickly add all the beans, and enjoy the song of searing vegetables in the pan. Do not mix or stir the beans for about 30 seconds—you want them to catch a good seared edge. Sprinkle with the salt and pepper. Cook for about 3 minutes, until the beans are getting some colour all around. Stir in the lemon juice. Cook until the beans are tender-crisp.

2 Transfer the beans to a serving bowl and garnish with the toasted almonds on top. Excellent choice!

Heydays Tip

To prepare the beans for cooking, trim the stems, then wash the beans. Allow them to dry off somewhat, as any water droplets will make little explosions when mixed with very hot oil. Let the beans hang out in a colander for an hour or so after cleaning and they will be good to go.

Dressed Beets with Dill

If you've never peeled beets that are still warm after boiling, have you even lived? Absurd questions aside, it's quite possible that you haven't done this, but it's a wonderful experience, and if they're red beets, it can result in a very macabre scene. They're earthy and sweet, and lend themselves beautifully to sour cream and dill—and just about anything, really. At home we have them with plain yogurt or a smattering of goat cheese. Just heavenly.

SERVES 4 TO 6

2 bunches of red beets (about 8 medium beets)
2 tbsp (30 mL) Lemon Vinaigrette (page 43)
½ bunch of fresh dill, fronds finely chopped (approx. 2 oz/55 g)
¼ cup (60 mL) finely chopped fresh chives (fin, fin, fin!)
¼ cup (60 mL) full-fat (14%) sour cream (optional)

1. Place the beets in a large pot of cold water and bring to a boil (the beets should be covered by at least 3 inches/8 cm of water). Reduce the heat to medium, and simmer until the beets are tender enough to stab with a fork with little to no resistance, 20 to 35 minutes, depending on the size of the beets.
2. Once cooked, drain the beets and let cool just until it's comfortable enough to handle them. While still warm, using your hands, peel the beets (gloves might not be a bad play here, as the beets will stain your hands pink; you can also use a kitchen towel that you don't mind staining red for the rest of its days).
3. Using a paring knife, cut the peeled beets into quarters, and place in a bowl with the vinaigrette. Toss until well coated.
4. Transfer the dressed beets to a serving dish. Sprinkle with the chopped dill and chives, and serve.
5. Add sour cream if you're feeling luxurious.

Heydays Fries

Freddy spent over a decade operating a poutine shop in Toronto before Heydays, so you could say that the humble spud is near and dear to his heart.

French fries are not the easiest thing to make at home, but we'll share our secrets in case you're up to the challenge.

Double-cooking fries in the Belgian method is essential. It ensures a crispy outside and a perfectly cooked inside. We like fine ground sea salt on our fries, so much so that we buy up cartons and cartons of our favourite brand every chance we get.

SERVES 4 TO 6

6 russet Burbank potatoes (If you can't find russet Burbank potatoes, plain russet or Yukon Gold potatoes work, too.)
16 cups (4 L) vegetable oil (a terrifying amount for residential cooking)
Sea salt

1 Leave the skin on the potatoes. With a chef's knife, very carefully cut the potatoes lengthwise into 3- to 4⅜-inch-thick (0.9 cm) sheets. (If you like gadgets, get a fry cutter and a ⅜ inch/0.9 cm die.) Then cut the sheets into ⅜-inch (0.9 cm) sticks.

2 In a deep pot over high heat, bring the oil to 310°F (154°C).

3 For the first fry (what we call the "blanching stage"), carefully drop one-third of the fries into the hot oil. Do not overcrowd. Then crank the heat to maximum (putting the fries in will reduce the heat), and set a timer for 3 minutes and 30 seconds. Monitor the heat of your oil pot and try to maintain a temperature as close to 310°F (154°C) as possible. Once the time is up, use a metal mesh spider strainer to remove the fries from the pot. Transfer the fries to a platter or baking sheet to cool. Repeat, in batches, with the remaining potatoes.

4 Ideally, the fries should have at least an hour to cool and get down to room temperature before going for their second bath in the oil.

5 Once all the fries have been blanched and cooled, heat the oil (cont'd)

in the pot to 350°F (180°C) over high heat for the final fry.

6 Working in batches, deep-fry the fries until nicely golden brown and crispy, 4 to 5 minutes. Again, once you drop the fries into the oil, crank the heat to full and monitor the temperature of the oil, aiming to maintain 350°F (180°C).

7 Once cooked, use the mesh spider strainer to transfer the fries to a metal bowl. Sprinkle the fries with sea salt and toss to coat. It takes a little getting used to, but tossing fries so they fly in the air and back into the bowl is a very pleasing rhythmic motion. But alas, a simple toss will suffice. Enjoy.

Savoury Sautéed Corn

Summer in our neck of the woods isn't really summer without fresh corn. While we have a soft spot for eating it right off the cob, with just butter and table salt like we did at Grandma's house, there is also a unique pleasure to be had when it's shaved into a delicious pile and doused in plenty of butter.

SERVES 4 TO 6

6 ears of fresh corn, husked
6 tbsp (90 mL) salted butter
2 tbsp (30 mL) finely diced shallots (brunoise)
2 tsp (10 mL) kosher salt
1 tsp (5 mL) freshly ground black pepper
3 tbsp (45 mL) finely chopped fresh flat-leaf parsley

1. In a medium shallow bowl, using a sharp knife, hold the corn upright and shave the kernels off the husk (you should get 4 nice cuts from top to bottom of the husk).

2. Heat a cast iron or heavy-bottomed pan over medium heat. Melt the butter and continue to heat it until it bubbles. Stir in the corn kernels, shallots, salt, and pepper. Sauté until the corn is nice and golden brown, 8 to 10 minutes. When you think it is just about done, add the parsley and stir around.

3. Divide evenly between your serving plates and top with an extra knob of butter.

Cocktail Party

We love the romantic nostalgia of getting dressed up for a night of endless passed snacks and an open bar. Heydays was born in the middle of the pandemic, when we were missing so many things, but there was a moment when we thought we might have seen the end of cocktail parties forever.

Imagine the sweet relief when we got to host a party for a very special regular Heydays guest—think rum cocktails with umbrellas, hors d'œuvres like Sliced Steak with Horseradish Mayo (page 215), Oyster Vodka Shooters (page 221), and a perfected favourite, our Classic Devilled Eggs (page 229). As odd as it sounds, that was the moment when things started to feel like they might be "normal" again—maybe even better than normal, thanks to the time we spent missing them.

What better reason to gather friends around to talk and laugh and eat than the simple fact that you can? So batch up the cocktails, don a dramatic cat-eye look, and get your share plate on!

COCKTAIL PARTY

The Bruce County Share Plate

Artfully styled charcuterie platters are certainly in vogue—and we love those salami roses, meticulously stacked cheeses, and grapes strewn throughout. However, we took a different route for elegant snacking and put a regionally inspired share plate on the menu. Called the Bruce County Share Plate, our version includes locally made Mennonite-style summer sausage, locally fished smoked trout, aged Canadian cheddar broken into chunks, and our Heydays Pickled Veg (page 208).

The pickled veg changes throughout the summer and is a beautiful way to showcase produce at its finest moment while adding a little acid to make the whole plate pop. The fish may change depending on the season and what's available, but you can replace it with a Smoked Fish Dip (page 61) if you like. We went with a cured meat that came from our area, and if we're honest, the summer sausage kept us alive the first couple of years running a busy restaurant. Evan had the idea for the rough chunks of cheddar that you can break up using an oyster knife if you want to (kind of like the Italians do to Parmesan with their tagliagrane, or special cheese knives meant for exactly this purpose). Add a bowl of our Marinated Warm Olives (page 211) to complete the whole thing.

JOURNA
ays serving good wine and good vib

Heydays Pickled Veg

While we haven't perfected the art of canning, we love what a light pickling can do to our local vegetables. In the springtime, we pickle our asparagus, and it makes for a perfect garnish for our Caesar (page 28) or Bloody Mary (page 26). As the summer carries on, we move on to green and yellow beans. Radishes and celery are a lovely part of our pickled veg medley, as is cauliflower—you name it, we've pickled it!

MAKES 4 CUPS (1 L) PICKED VEGETABLES

8 cups (2 L) water
1 cup (240 mL) white vinegar
6½ tbsp (95 g) kosher salt (see Heydays Tip)
6 cloves of garlic
1 tsp (5 mL) chili flakes
1 bunch of fresh dill (approx. 3½ oz/100 g)
1 cup (250 mL) cauliflower florets
1 cup (250 mL) sliced carrots
1 cup (250 mL) sliced fennel
1 cup (250 mL) sliced celery root

1. In a medium pot, combine the water, vinegar, salt, garlic, and chili flakes. Bring to a boil.

2. Place the dill, cauliflower, carrots, fennel, and celery root in a large canning jar or a plastic container that is narrow enough to ensure that all the vegetables are covered by the boiling-hot pickle brine.

3. Pour the boiling pickle brine over the vegetables. You might have a bit of extra brine; just ensure that the garlic and chili flakes make it into the container. Let sit, uncovered, at room temperature until it has cooled.

4. Once cool, cover with a lid and store in the fridge. Allow the pickles to marinate for at least 24 hours to get the full effect of the brine.

5. The pickled vegetables will last at least a month in the fridge. Enjoy!

Heydays Tip

This recipe was tested using Diamond Crystal kosher salt. Not all kosher salts have the same level of saltiness, so take that into consideration. We also recommend using salt by weight for this recipe to achieve a better result.

Marinated Warm Olives

Olives are nice, but warm olives are better. We find these the perfect accompaniment to an Old Fashioned (page 18) and an elegant little touch to your share plate. We prefer to serve them with pits because they tend to retain their structure better, and we've had enough poorly pitted olives to know that it's probably better to expect a pit and eat around it than gleefully chomp into one by accident. There's probably a metaphor for life in there, somewhere.

¼ cup (60 mL) olive oil
12 cloves garlic
1 cup (250 mL) kalamata olives, with pits
1 cup (250 mL) Castelvetrano olives, with pits (see Heydays Tip, page 74)
Large orange rind slices from 1 orange (like you'd make to garnish an Old Fashioned, page 18)
12 sprigs fresh thyme
2 sprigs fresh rosemary
2 fresh bay leaves

1 In a small pan over medium heat, combine the oil and garlic. Let them cook gently for about 8 minutes, until the cloves have softened and everything is smelling delicious. Add the olives, orange rinds, thyme, rosemary, and bay leaves. Cook, stirring occasionally, until everything is warmed through, for about another 4 minutes. (Don't stir too vigorously or you might break up your olives.)

2 Serve with a small side bowl for pits.

Potato Cheddar Croquettes

These wee croquettes are just a whole lot of fun, so we thought they deserved to be showcased. Once again, they were made from ingredients we already had on hand but adapted, as though we said, "Potatoes, but make it a party." Maybe the lesson here is to always have potatoes on hand ... This is also an ideal recipe for leftover mashed potatoes.

MAKES ABOUT 20 CROQUETTES

- **4 large russet potatoes, peeled and cubed**
- **3 tbsp (45 mL) kosher salt, divided**
- **½ cup (125 mL) salted butter**
- **1½ cups (375 mL) homogenized (3.25%) milk**
- **4 egg yolks**
- **2 cups (500 mL) shredded cheddar cheese**
- **1½ cups (375 mL) all-purpose flour**
- **3 whole eggs, beaten**
- **2 cups (500 mL) plain panko crumbs**
- **Vegetable oil, for frying**
- **Sea salt, to taste**
- **Lemon Old Bay Sauce (page 214), for serving**
- **sea salt, for serving**

1. Put the potatoes in a medium pot and cover with cold water. Add 2 tbsp (30 mL) of the salt. Place the pot over high heat and bring to a boil. Once boiling, reduce the heat to medium and simmer for 20 to 30 minutes, or until the potatoes are completely cooked through and fork-tender.

2. Meanwhile, in a small pot over medium heat, melt the butter. Then add the milk and stir quite often until the milk is hot (be careful not to scald the milk).

3. Once the potatoes are cooked, strain and return to the pot. Using a potato masher, mash the potatoes. Add half of the hot buttery milk, and continue mashing. Add the remaining milk, and continue mashing/stirring. Add the remaining 1 tbsp (15 mL) of salt. Taste the mash and add more salt, if needed. Refrigerate the mashed potatoes until they are cool to the touch, about 1 hour.

4. Once the potatoes have cooled, add the egg yolks and cheese. Stir to incorporate.

5. Line a baking sheet with parchment paper. Using your hands, shape the mashed potatoes into little balls (nice golf ball–size pieces are ideal) and place on your prepared baking sheet. Chill in the fridge for about another hour. (cont'd)

6 Set up a breading station with 3 shallow bowls: one for the flour, one for the beaten eggs, and one for the panko.

7 Working with one chilled potato ball at a time, roll in the flour first, then the egg wash, and then the panko. Return to the baking sheet, and then repeat until all of the balls are breaded. Fill a heavy-bottomed pot or deep cast iron pan with ½ inch (1 cm) of oil. Place over medium-high heat, and heat to 350°F (180°C).

8 Carefully place 6 to 8 croquettes in the hot oil. Do not overcrowd the pan. Cook the croquettes for 6 to 7 minutes, or until golden brown. Flip and cook the other side for another 6 to 7 minutes. Using a slotted spoon or spider, carefully transfer the croquettes onto a paper towel–lined baking sheet. Repeat until all of the croquettes are cooked.

9 Dust the croquettes with sea salt. Serve hot with the Lemon Old Bay Sauce on the side. Enjoy!

Lemon Old Bay Sauce

This simple sauce is a bright accompaniment to the Potato Croquettes and, with its combination of lemon, Old Bay, and fresh herbs, also manages to create a common thread with so many of our other dishes. Use it for everything.

MAKES ABOUT 2 CUPS (500 ML)

1 cup (250 mL) mayonnaise
1 cup (250 mL) full-fat (14%) sour cream
Zest of 1 lemon
Juice of 1 lemon
1 tbsp (15 mL) Old Bay Seasoning
¼ bunch of fresh chives, finely chopped (fin, fin, fin!) (approx. ½ oz/15 g)

1 In a mixing bowl and using a rubber spatula, stir together the mayo, sour cream, lemon zest and juice, and Old Bay. Transfer to a serving bowl and garnish with the chives. Refrigerate until ready to serve. This can be made up to a week in advance.

Sliced Steak with Horseradish Mayo

Just as a steak dinner is a lovely way to commemorate a special occasion, slicing a steak to serve over baguette and horseradish mayo feels like a party. Use a tender cut and thinly slice so the steak can be eaten easily from one hand while holding a classic cocktail in the other.

MAKES 15 TO 20 PIECES

1 x 14- to 16-oz (400 g to 450 g) New York striploin, nice and thick (1 inch/2.5 cm or more), or 2 x 8-oz (225 g) filets mignon
1 tbsp (15 mL) kosher salt
1 tbsp (15 mL) freshly cracked black pepper
2 tbsp (30 mL) olive oil
¼ cup (60 mL) salted butter, at room temperature + extra for toasting the bread
3 cloves of garlic in their husk (unpeeled)
5 sprigs fresh thyme
Maldon Salt, to taste
1 cup (250 mL) Horseradish Mayo (page 216)
1 fresh baguette, sliced on an angle about ½ inch (1 cm) thick

1. Heat a cast iron or heavy-bottomed pan over medium-high heat until it is screaming hot.

2. Pat the steak dry with a paper towel. Season all sides with salt and pepper (the steak should be fairly aggressively seasoned). Lather the steak with the olive oil—there is no need to put oil into the pan. Place the steak in your hot pan, laying it away from you. Relish in the sound of the sizzle. Reduce the heat to medium-high. Sear the steak until nicely browned, about 4 minutes.

3. Flip the steak and continue searing for an additional 2 minutes, until nicely browned on each side.

4. Add the butter, garlic, and thyme to the pan. Once the butter has melted, use a nice long-handled spoon to baste the steak continuously. Flip the steak over and baste, repeating several times. The ideal cook for the steak is medium-rare, or an internal temperature of 130°F (55°C). Keep in mind that the steak's temperature will continue to increase 5 to 10 degrees after it has been removed from the pan.

5. Remove the steak from the pan and let rest on a cutting board for about 8 minutes before slicing.

6. Using a sharp knife, slice the steak fairly thinly, enough to get about 15 slices per striploin or 8 to 10 slices per fillet. (cont'd)

7 Place a frying pan over medium heat.

8 Using a bread knife, cut the baguette on an angle to get nice ½ inch (1 cm) slices. Spread both sides of each slice with a light coating of butter. Working in batches, toast the bread until nicely golden brown on each side. Arrange the pieces of baguette in a row on a serving plate.

9 Spread a generous portion of Horseradish Mayo on each piece of bread. Place a slice of steak on each piece of bread. Sprinkle with Maldon Salt. Pass and enjoy!

Horseradish Mayo

Horseradish and steak is a classic combination, but that sharp brightness from horseradish also ties in some of our restaurant's seafood themes. This simple recipe is an easy way to dress up this passed appetizer.

MAKES ABOUT 1½ CUPS (375 ML)

1 cup (250 mL) mayonnaise
½ cup (125 mL) prepared horseradish
1 tsp (5 mL) kosher salt
1 tsp (5 mL) freshly cracked black pepper

1 In a small bowl, stir together the mayo, horseradish, salt, and pepper. Cover and refrigerate until needed. It will keep for up to a week.

Oysters Rockefeller

At Heydays, we prefer fresh, coldwater oysters. They get nicely plump, and there's a clarity to the brine in the shell. That said, there is something wonderfully retro about baked oysters, and we love the mystery surrounding the original recipe developed by Antoine's in New Orleans—arguably the home of Oysters Rockefeller.

We decided to top ours with the hollandaise sauce that we have on hand during brunch service, and then a piece of bacon. The result is rich and delicious, but balanced enough to make us forget about fresh, briny oysters for just a moment.

MAKES 18 OYSTERS

½ cup (125 mL) salted butter, softened (leave it out overnight)
3 cloves of garlic, finely minced (use a kitchen rasp)
½ cup (125 mL) finely chopped fresh flat-leaf parsley
4 strips bacon
Rock salt, for serving
18 East Coast oysters
½ cup (125 mL) Heydays Hollandaise (page 246)

1. Preheat your oven to 350°F (180°C). Line a baking sheet with parchment paper.

2. In a small bowl, using a rubber spatula, stir together the butter, parsley, and garlic.

3. Arrange the bacon in a single layer on your prepared baking sheet. Cook the bacon in your preheated oven for 15 minutes, and then flip it over and cook for another 10 minutes, or until desired crispiness is achieved. Drain the bacon on paper towels after cooking. Once cooled, cut into bite-size pieces.

4. Increase the oven temperature to 400°F (200°C). Line a baking sheet with ¼ inch (½ cm) of rock salt.

5. Shuck the oysters and arrange in a single layer on the bed of salt (this prevents the oysters from tipping over while they're cooking; it doesn't really do anything from a flavour perspective). Place ½ tbsp (7 mL) of the herbed butter on each oyster.

6. Bake the oysters until cooked through, about 7 minutes (at this point they should have lost their shine and started to firm up). Remove the pan from the oven. Change the oven (cont'd)

temperature to a high broil. Spoon ½ tbsp (7 mL) of hollandaise onto each oyster. Return the pan to the oven, and bake the oysters just until the hollandaise begins to brown, about 30 seconds.

7 Arrange the baked oysters on a serving platter lined with more rock salt. Add a few pieces of bacon per oyster. Enjoy hot!

Oyster Vodka Shooters

Nothing says cocktail party like vodka and oysters! The vodka tends to be a perfect pairing with the brininess of the oyster, and just a little bit of heat, whether from our Heydays Hot Sauce (page 44) or Cocktail Sauce (page 38), is a brilliant combination.

It is very important to keep everything cold as you work: keep the oysters on a tray of shaved ice, and be sure to pop your bottle of vodka in the freezer the night before (nobody wants to drink warm vodka, with oysters or otherwise).

MAKES 1 SHOOTER (REPEAT AS MANY TIMES AS NEEDED)

1 freshly shucked oyster (page 35)
1 tsp (5 mL) vodka
1 tsp (5 mL) Cocktail Sauce (page 38)
Heydays Hot Sauce (page 44), to taste

1. Arrange your shot glasses on a tray. Spoon the Heydays Cocktail Sauce into the bottom of each one, and then chill them in the fridge while you shuck the oysters.

2. Shuck your oysters first, keeping them on a tray of shaved ice as you work.

3. Slide an oyster into each shot glass and refrigerate until ready to serve.

4. Once ready to serve, pour a dash of vodka into each shot glass (really, just enough to taste). Put out a small bowl of hot sauce so people can add heat as desired.

Heydays Tip

Another way of serving this is as a passed hors d'oeuvre, à la Freddy. Shuck your oysters and lay them out on a tray of shaved ice. Toss a small bowl of Heydays Hot Sauce in the ice as well. Make sure you have a towel for the hand holding the freezing oyster tray. In your dominant hand, take the bottle of vodka (adding a pour spout is helpful, or put the vodka into a little vinegar bottle or cruet). Once you have found a willing participant, splash some vodka on their oyster and encourage them to dress it up with hot sauce and cocktail sauce, as needed.

STURGEON CAVIAR
ACADIAN EMERALD
New Brunswick, Canada, www.acadian-sturgeon.com
Acadian Caviar
Acadian Caviar

Caviar, Blinis & the Fixin's

We experienced our first caviar service at a local oyster restaurant. It was the first time we saw the sweet little piles of shaved hard-boiled egg, the whites and the yolks separated, joined by piles of finely diced shallots and crème fraîche.

While caviar can certainly come off as pretentious, it can also be so much fun, and we love to use Canadian caviar, which is delicious, local, and far more affordable than its Russian cousins.

We told our caviar supplier that we were including his caviar in this book and that we were doing it in the traditional style with all the "fixin's." He very passionately exclaimed: "No! Those toppings were meant to hide bad caviar. You must eat a little spoonful by itself!" So just know that's an option, too.

SERVES 4 CAVIAR LOVERS OR 8 CAVIAR CURIOUS

1 oz (30 g) tin of caviar (we prefer Acadian Sturgeon Caviar)
20 fresh Buckwheat Blinis (page 224)
4 hard-boiled eggs, egg whites separated from the yolks
2 tbsp (30 mL) finely diced shallots (brunoise)
½ cup (125 mL) Countertop Crème Fraîche (page 225)
3 tbsp (45 mL) finely chopped fresh chives (fin, fin, fin!)

1. Use a kitchen rasp to shave the egg whites first and then the egg yolks (they may crumble a bit, but that's okay; they're meant to be a topping).

2. Arrange the shaved egg whites and egg yolks, shallots, crème fraîche, and chives in small piles on your serving platter. Crush up some ice and place in a bowl on which to rest your caviar tin.

3. Invite your guests to build their own blini. We recommend caviar first, and then a little bit of everything on top. Or build the blinis for your guests. We like a scoop of caviar, a sprinkle of shallots, crème fraîche, and a chive garnish.

Buckwheat Blinis

We once went on a birthday picnic where the host was so well-prepared, he had blini mix in a squeeze bottle and dotted blinis into a pan cooked over a camp stove. He brought little pots of crème fraîche, and then produced small cans of fish roe for a picnic caviar service. It might have been the coolest thing we've ever seen, and we definitely stole the squeeze bottle idea.

MAKES 20 TO 30 BLINIS, DEPENDING ON SIZE

1 cup (250 mL) buckwheat flour
½ cup (125 mL) all-purpose flour
2 tsp (10 mL) granulated sugar
½ tsp (2 mL) kosher salt
½ tsp (2 mL) baking powder
¼ tsp (1 mL) baking soda
2 cups (500 mL) buttermilk
2 tbsp (30 mL) unsalted butter, melted
2 large eggs, separated
1 tbsp (15 mL) vegetable oil + more for cooking

1. In a bowl, whisk together the flours, sugar, kosher salt, baking powder, and baking soda.

2. In another bowl, whisk together the buttermilk, melted butter, and egg yolks. Add this to your flour mixture, and stir until just combined. Set aside.

3. You now need to whip the egg whites to stiff peaks (the air that the whites can hold rivals that of any you could get from yeast, and this cuts down on the time it takes to prepare, really!). Fold the egg whites into the batter and stir until just combined.

4. For restaurant-style precision, transfer the batter to a squeeze bottle with a tip that has been cut a little wider than normal (this can be great for keeping Heydays Dijonnaise, page 135, or Caesar dressing, page 87, on hand as well).

5. Place a non-stick pan that has been lightly coated in oil over medium heat. Once the pan is hot, use your squeeze bottle to dot small circles of batter about the size of a Canadian toonie or an American silver dollar into the pan. Once the tops of the blini start to lose their shine (after 3 to 4 minutes), flip them over and cook for another minute. Repeat with the remaining batter, then keep the cooked blinis in a warm oven until ready to serve.

Countertop Crème Fraîche

Store-bought crème fraîche can be lovely, but we were fascinated to learn that this method works really well. It took a little longer than expected the first time—we suspect that it might be particularly sensitive to environmental variables—but it's fun to play around with the texture of this version. Enjoy this on top of the Buckwheat Blinis or as the base for a dip.

MAKES ABOUT 1 CUP (250 ML)

1 cup (250 mL) heavy (whipping) cream
$1\frac{1}{2}$ tbsp (22 mL) buttermilk

1. In a glass jar, combine the heavy cream and buttermilk. Cover with plastic wrap and leave on the countertop at room temperature overnight or for 18 hours.

2. Check consistency: you're looking for it to resemble sour cream. Leave it on the counter for an additional couple hours, if needed.

3. To stop the thickening process, place a lid on the crème and refrigerate it. Crème fraîche will keep in the fridge for about a week.

Oysters Royale

When we finally ordered the caviar at our favourite little oyster bar, our server, Tyler, told us to try a little bit on an oyster. He called it an Oyster Royale. It was an umami explosion that felt like the height of decadence, so we include it here, for that moment when you just happen to have oysters and caviar on hand. Just put a little spoonful of caviar on top of the oyster with nothing else. Scouring the internet reveals little about the origins of the Oyster Royale. It's possible that Tyler made it up. We share it with you because, as we say, it would be rude not to.

SERVES 4

12 fresh oysters
2 lb (900 g) crushed or shaved ice, on a serving tray
1 oz (30 g) tin of caviar (we prefer Acadian Sturgeon Caviar)
2 oyster lemons (page 43)

1. Shuck the oysters, and then nestle them into the crushed ice. Scoop about $\frac{1}{4}$ tsp (1 mL) of the caviar onto each oyster. Serve with oyster lemons, and enjoy!

Classic Devilled Eggs

Rather than cut the egg lengthwise, we cut it in half around the middle and then slice off a little bit of the ends so there's a flat surface for these little cups to sit on.

The word "devilled" describes foods that have some spice to them, and in our case it's Dijon mustard and Old Bay Seasoning. We added Old Bay Seasoning to our egg yolk mix, as it is in keeping with the flavours of Heydays. These eggs are at home beside our Old Bay Fried Chicken (page 158), which might leave your guests pondering the perennial question, What came first, the fried chicken or the devilled egg?

MAKES 24 HALVES

12 large eggs
2 tbsp (30 mL) baking soda
1½ tsp (7 mL) freshly ground black pepper
1½ tsp (7 mL) Old Bay Seasoning
½ cup (125 mL) mayonnaise
1 tbsp (15 mL) Dijon mustard
¼ cup (60 mL) finely chopped fresh chives (fin, fin, fin!)
1 tbsp (15 mL) capers, drained and chopped

1. Place the eggs in a large stockpot. Cover with about 3 inches (8 cm) of water, and add the baking soda.

2. Put over high heat, cover with the lid, and bring to a boil. Once the water is boiling, remove the pan from the heat and let stand, covered, for 10 minutes.

3. Peel and rinse the eggs. Using a paring knife, cut a tiny bit off each end so the egg halves can sit flat, upright. Then cut the eggs widthwise down the centre (not lengthwise, as is traditional).

4. Scoop out both yolk halves and transfer to a medium bowl. Set aside your egg cups.

5. Stir the yolk mixture until smooth, and then fold in pepper, Old Bay, mayo, mustard, chives, and capers until completely incorporated. Spoon into a resealable bag and seal. Cut a small corner from the bag, twist the bag to force the egg into the corner, and pipe the filling into the eggs. (You can use a piping bag and star attachment, but we actually normally use a resealable bag.) As you pipe, hold the tip of the bag very close to the base of the egg and, squeezing firmly and quickly, let the yolk mix fold in over itself until it's a small dome. Like flipping a potato rösti (see Heydays Tip, page 238), it's more about commitment than skill. (cont'd)

6 Finish with a slight sprinkle of Old Bay, but remember, there's salt in there, so don't go too crazy with it. Enjoy in a single bite!

Heydays Tip

You probably know how to boil an egg, but we still like to share this trick because we think a lot of eggs in the world get over-boiled and end up with that unappealing greenish tinge on the yolk that tastes a little bit like chalk.

Place your eggs in a pot, and then cover with water—the water should be about 1 inch (2.5 cm) above your eggs. Put the pot over high heat, and bring the water to a boil, uncovered. Once boiling, take the pot off the heat and set a timer for 10 minutes (leave the pot uncovered). Once the timer goes off, run the eggs under cold water so they stop cooking. You end up with a beautiful, just-done yolk inside that is really delicious to eat with a bit of Maldon Salt or a dollop of our Heydays Dijonnaise (page 135).

Brunch

SHALLOW AREA

It's quite possible that the only thing better than a poolside lunch is a poolside brunch.

You start the morning with a swim—maybe you're feeling a little foggy, but it's nothing that a quick dip can't solve. The sun is already getting hot by the time you climb out of the pool, so you order a Mimosa (page 25). Somehow, feeling a little better makes you hungry. You grab a menu and lean back in a lounge chair to peruse the offerings.

Today is going to be a good day.

BRUNCH

Two-Potato Rösti

with Smoked Fish, Sour Cream & Chives

We ended up with a lot of potatoes at home as we were menu planning at the very beginning of the pandemic. This was our favourite recipe to come out of that strange time. It's less about the ingredients, which are simple, and more about the technique. The result is a delicious, crispy potato rösti that can be made for any meal. We like it with local smoked fish, our Countertop Crème Fraîche (page 225), and chives, but we also serve it with sunny-side-up eggs and as a side for steak or, frankly, just about anything.

SERVES 2 TO 4

2 large Russet potatoes, peeled
2½ tsp (12 mL) kosher salt
3 tbsp (45 mL) salted butter
2 tbsp (30 mL) olive oil
7 oz (200 g) hot-smoked fish
½ cup (125 mL) full-fat (14%) sour cream
1 tbsp (15 mL) finely chopped fresh chives (fin, fin, fin!)

1 Using the large holes of a cheese grater, grate the potatoes on their long side (if you get some smaller strands of potato, that is completely fine, but aim to get some nice long strands). Place in a large bowl. Stir the salt into the potatoes and let them sit for about 10 minutes (we are extracting water from the potatoes, and the salt does a bang-up job doing that).

2 One handful at a time, ball up the grated potato and squeeze out as much excess water as you can and then transfer to a new bowl.

3 Place a large nonstick pan over medium heat. Melt the butter in the oil, and heat until the butter gets frothy. Arrange all of the grated potato evenly over the base of the pan and, using a rubber spatula, gently press it into a pancake-like form until it's no more than ½ inch (1 cm) thick. Cook until the top of the grated potatoes becomes translucent, about 10 minutes.

4 Big moment here: it's time for the flip. It is most exhilarating if done by tossing the rösti into the air and catching it back in the pan. We usually do this over the sink in case of any accidents. Otherwise, flip it with the help of two spatulas. Either way, it's a bit tricky. Good luck and have fun! (cont'd)

5 Once safely flipped, cook the other side until golden brown, about 7 minutes. Gently slide the rösti onto a cutting board and, using a sharp knife, cut it into four equal pieces.

6 Garnish each slice of rösti with 1.7 oz (50 g) of the smoked fish, topped with 2 tbsp (30 mL) of the sour cream and a good sprinkling of chives. Please enjoy!

Heydays Tip

Mastering the rösti flip is also a fun party trick. It's important to let the rösti cook for longer than you probably think it should. As long as the temperature on the pan isn't too high, the bottom will get crispy while slowly cooking off the water in the potato. Once the rösti is nicely brown when you lift up the edge with a spatula, it's time to flip it. We recommend using a non-stick frying pan with a low edge and maybe doing it over the sink the first time. Just remember: like most things in life, a good rösti flip is more about commitment than skill.

Eggs Benedict Four Ways

One of the formative places we worked at prior to opening Heydays was a golf club in the States. For one particular tournament there was always an eggs Benedict buffet in the morning before tee-off. We love a classic Benny but decided to offer it a few ways: with the same lobster-shallot mix from our Hot Lobster Roll (page 129) or with spinach, smoked salmon, or bacon. In Canada, it's common to see peameal bacon on an eggs Benny, but we stuck with strip bacon, mostly so we could use it on our burgers, too.

Perfectly Poached Eggs

Making a perfectly poached egg was oddly intimidating at first—the way the eggs are at risk of breaking up in the water, not knowing how well they're cooked through, the horror of transporting them ... So we're sharing the secrets we picked up after many years of making and serving brunch!

SERVES 2

32 cups (8 L) water
¼ cup (60 mL) white vinegar
4 large eggs

1. In a large saucepan, bring the water to a boil. Once boiling, add the white vinegar. Reduce the heat to medium-low.

2. Crack each egg into a little bowl or cup, and ensure there is no broken shell in there.

3. Using a long spoon, stir the water in the pan in a circular manner to get a vortex going. At this point, the water should be super hot, maybe a few little simmering bubbles, but not boiling.

4. Quickly and efficiently, drop in each egg, just slightly off centre of the vortex. The purpose of the vortex is to assist the egg white to wrap around itself and create a beautiful pillowy egg.

5. To make a nice rich and runny egg, you will need to poach for 3 to 4 minutes (you can test the eggs by gently tapping them to see if they spring back a little). Use a slotted spoon to transfer the eggs to a clean kitchen towel to drain.

Classic Eggs Benny

This is the classic and our most popular version. Some schools of thought would have you using pea-meal bacon ("Canadian bacon" in the US), but we are firm backers of strip bacon—it has that extra crispy, salty decadence that we all need when on vacation.

SERVES 2

2 English muffins
Salted butter, at room temperature, for spreading
4 slices cooked bacon, cut in half widthwise
4 large eggs, poached (page 239)
Heydays Hollandaise, for serving (page 246)
Finely chopped fresh chives, for garnish (fin, fin, fin!)

1 Unless they come pre-sliced, cut the English muffins in half with a serrated knife. Lightly slather each cut side with butter. Place a pan over medium heat, and toast the buttered side of each muffin until golden brown. Set aside.

2 Poach your eggs and lay them on a clean kitchen towel while you assemble the rest of your Benedicts.

3 Arrange two sides of the toasted English muffins on each plate.

4 Top each side with two half-slices of cooked bacon, add your poached eggs (carefully!); and then follow that with the Heydays Hollandaise. Garnish with the herb of your choice. At Heydays, it's the finely cut chives on the classic Benny.

Lobster Benedict

This is really just our Hot Lobster Roll (page 129) ... but make it breakfast. You're going to do just the same thing you do to make a lobster roll, but then layer hot lobster over the English muffins and top them with a poached egg and Heydays Hollandaise (page 246). These flavours go so well together!

SERVES 2

4 large eggs, poached (page 239)
2 English muffins, split and toasted (page 240)
1 tbsp (15 mL) finely diced shallots (brunoise)
¼ cup (60 mL) salted butter
7 oz (200 g) lobster meat
Heydays Hollandaise, for serving (page 246)
1 tbsp (15 mL) fresh tarragon leaves

1. Poach your eggs and lay them on a clean kitchen towel while you assemble the rest of your Benedicts.

2. Toast your English muffins.

3. Place a pan over medium heat. Add the butter and shallots, and cook, stirring occasionally, for 2 minutes, until the shallots are translucent. Add the lobster meat, and cook, stirring gently, for about 1 minute.

4. Using a slotted spoon, divide the lobster meat between 4 pieces of toasted English muffins. Gently place a poached egg onto each muffin. Top with Heydays Hollandaise, and then tarragon. Enjoy!

Spinach Benedict

We used to put this spinach mix on a yearly New Year's Day breakfast poutine. Something about spinach makes everything feel healthier, so here is our attempt. And it just happens to be delicious when covered in egg and Heydays Hollandaise (page 246), too.

SERVES 2

4 large eggs, poached (page 239)
2 English muffins, split and toasted (page 240)
2 tbsp (30 mL) olive oil
7 oz (200 g) fresh spinach
2 tbsp (30 mL) finely diced shallots (brunoise)
1 tsp (5 mL) kosher salt
1 tsp (5 mL) freshly cracked black pepper
2 tbsp (30 mL) dry white wine
Heydays Hollandaise (page 246), for serving
1 tbsp (15 mL) finely chopped fresh flat-leaf parsley, for garnish

1. Poach your eggs and lay them on a clean kitchen towel while you assemble the rest of your Benedicts.

2. Toast your English muffins.

3. Heat a large steel pan over medium-high heat. Add the olive oil, and heat until it shimmers. Add the spinach, and cook for about 30 seconds, until it is crisp and crackles. Add the shallots, salt, and pepper. Stir that around a bit. Add the white wine, and cook for about 30 seconds, until the wine has mostly evaporated and the spinach is nicely wilted.

4. Divide the spinach between your toasted English muffins, arranging it into little nests. Nestle a poached egg into each nest and top with Heydays Hollandaise and chopped parsley. Enjoy!

Smoked Salmon Benedict

Always a classic eggs Benedict option, smoked salmon benny needed to be included in our brunch menu. It's just perfect, and we love it with fresh dill.

SERVES 2

4 large eggs, poached (page 239)
2 English muffins, split and toasted (page 240)
3½ oz (100 g) cold-smoked salmon, or 4 nice slices
1 tbsp (15 mL) finely diced shallots (brunoise)
Heydays Hollandaise (page 246), for serving
1 tbsp (15 mL) roughly chopped fresh dill fronds, for garnish

1. Poach your eggs and lay them on a clean kitchen towel while you assemble the rest of your Benedicts.
2. Toast your English muffins.
3. Divide the salmon between 4 toasted slices of English muffin. Top with equal amounts of diced shallots. Gently place a perfectly poached egg on each one. Top with Heydays Hollandaise. Garnish with fresh dill. Enjoy!

Heydays Hollandaise

One of our favourite things about our Benny is the foolproof hollandaise we developed after a lot of research. This hollandaise skips the constant whisking over hot water in favour of a blender.

MAKES 2½ CUPS (625 ML)

1 lb (454 g) salted butter
6 large egg yolks
1 tbsp (15 mL) fresh lemon juice
2 tbsp (30 mL) hot water
Pinch of cayenne pepper

1. In a saucepan, melt the butter and heat to 190°F (87°C). Transfer the melted butter to a pitcher or other container you feel comfortable using to pour slowly.

2. In a Vitamix or blender, combine the egg yolks, lemon juice, hot water, and cayenne pepper.

3. Blend on low speed. Gradually add the melted butter, leaving the white residue/milk solids behind (the milk solids should remain at the bottom). Once you have put all the butter in, crank the power on the blender to halfway and blend until the mixture emulsifies into a nice thick sauce, about 2 minutes. If it is too thick, add a ½ tbsp (7 mL) of water at a time and stir (not blend) to reach desired thickness. If it is too thin, add another egg yolk and blend for 10 seconds.

4. Transfer your hollandaise sauce to a holding vessel (we like a squeeze bottle) and store in a warm water bath of no more than 130°F (54°C) until ready to use. Refresh the warm water bath as needed.

Home Fries

We're after simple, easy home fries, but here's the trick: baking soda helps make them crispy and delicious. In science terms, it raises the alkalinity; in our terms, they're fluffier and better. At the restaurant, a little vinegar introduced at the blanching stage helps them stay together in the fryer, but we do the opposite at home.

SERVES 4

16 cups (4 L) water (enough to cover cubed potatoes)
4 large russet potatoes, cut into ¾-inch (2 cm) cubes
3 tbsp (45 mL) kosher salt, for blanching
1 tbsp (15 mL) baking soda
¼ cup (60 mL) olive oil
2 tsp (10 mL) sea salt
Mayonnaise or Heydays Dijonnaise (page 135) for serving

1 The first step to crispy and delicious home fries is water blanching. In a large pot, combine the water, cubed potatoes, kosher salt, and baking soda. Bring to a boil and cook the potatoes until fork-tender, about 45 minutes.

2 Preheat your oven to 450°F (230°C). Line a baking sheet with parchment paper.

3 Once the potatoes are cooked, strain and then arrange in a single layer on a tray to cool for 10 minutes.

4 In a large bowl, toss your soon-to-be home fries with the olive oil and sea salt. Arrange in a single layer on your prepared baking sheet. Pop into the hot oven and bake for 20 minutes. Remove the pan from the oven, stir the potatoes, and return the pan to the oven. Bake for an additional 10 minutes, or until the home fries are golden brown and crispy. Enjoy with a side of mayonnaise or class it up with some Heydays Dijonnaise!

Heydays Granola

We're not very good at healthy breakfast. We usually leave that to our friends up the road at The Wellness Refinery, where the motel guests go to get smoothies, smoothie bowls, and delicious toasts. That said, we knew we had to have one brunch option that was a little on the healthier side, so we started making our own granola. It's so fun to make this at home, and using local maple syrup to sweeten it feels special.

MAKES ABOUT 4 CUPS (1 L)

½ cup (125 mL) coconut oil, melted
½ cup (125 mL) pure maple syrup
1 tsp (5 mL) pure vanilla extract
4 cups (1 L) rolled oats
1 cup (250 mL) sliced almonds
1 cup (250 mL) roasted pepita seeds
1 tsp (5 mL) sea salt
½ tsp (2 mL) ground cinnamon
1 cup (250 mL) dried unsweetened cranberries

1. Preheat your oven to 350°F (180°C). Line a baking sheet with parchment paper.

2. In a bowl, whisk together the melted coconut oil, maple syrup, and vanilla. Add the oats, sliced almonds, pepitas, salt, and cinnamon.

3. Spread the mixture over your prepared baking sheet and bake for 24 minutes, until nicely toasted. Remove the pan from the oven, and let cool completely.

4. Once cool, stir in dried cranberries. This granola will keep in a resealable container at room temperature for up to 2 weeks.

Buttermilk Pancakes

We wanted to put a very classic pancake on our brunch menu but also wanted to make sure it wasn't the kind that would weigh you down at the beach, because that's where everyone is headed after a brunch at Heydays! We combined a couple of recipes, but ultimately opted for what is called a soufflé-style pancake. All that means is that you separate the eggs and beat the egg whites prior to folding them into the batter. This batter comes out a little more scraggly than a traditional pancake batter, but the result is a fluffy and delicious pancake that you can enjoy poolside.

SERVES 4

2 cups (500 mL) all-purpose flour
1 tsp (5 mL) baking powder
½ tsp (2 mL) baking soda
1½ tsp (7 mL) kosher salt
1 tbsp (15 mL) granulated sugar
2 large egg yolks (reserve the egg whites)
1¼ cups (300 mL) buttermilk
½ cup (125 mL) full-fat (14%) sour cream
¼ cup (60 mL) salted butter, melted
Maple Chantilly Cream (page 252), for serving
Candied Pecans (page 252), for serving
Spiced Maple Syrup (page 252), for serving

1. In a large bowl, stir together the flour, baking powder, baking soda, salt, and sugar.
2. In another bowl, beat the egg whites into stiff peaks and set aside.
3. In a third bowl, stir together the egg yolks, buttermilk, sour cream, and melted butter. Add to the dry ingredients in the large bowl and stir until just combined. Do not overstir—you are simply looking to incorporate the ingredients. Using a spatula, gently fold the stiff egg whites into the batter.
4. Put a large non-stick frying pan over medium-low heat. Melt 1 tbsp (15 mL) of the butter. Once the butter is bubbling, you can begin cooking pancakes.
5. Ladle the batter into the hot pan (ideally, a ⅓ cup/75 mL portion of batter makes a nice-sized pancake). Let the pancake cook until you see little bubbles form on top, 5 to 7 minutes. Carefully flip the pancake, and cook the other side for an additional 5 to 7 minutes. Check for doneness by inserting a toothpick into the side: if no batter stays stuck to it, the pancake is ready.
6. Top your pancake with your choice of butter, fresh fruit, Maple Chantilly Cream, Candied Pecans, or Spiced Maple Syrup.

Maple Chantilly Cream

Chantilly cream is really just a fancy way to say sweetened whipped cream. Because we're Canadian, we like to use maple syrup.

MAKES A HEAPING 2 CUPS (500 ML)

2 cups (500 mL) heavy (whipping) cream

2 tbsp (30 mL) pure maple syrup

1 In a stand mixer fitted with the whisk attachment, on medium speed, whisk together the heavy cream and maple syrup until soft peaks form. We recommend making this just before serving and using it all up!

Candied Pecans

Pecans add some complex nuttiness to a dish. We love the way they round out sweet breakfast treats.

MAKES 2 CUPS (500 ML)

½ cup (125 mL) granulated sugar

½ cup (125 mL) brown sugar, lightly packed

1 tsp (5 mL) ground cinnamon

2 cups (500 mL) halved pecans

1 In a medium pot over medium heat, heat the sugars until they begin to melt and caramelize. Add the pecans and cinnamon, and stir until well incorporated. Once the whole mixture is thoroughly combined, pour out and evenly spread onto a parchment-lined baking sheet. Let cool for an hour (minimum). These will keep for up to a week in a resealable container at room temperature.

Spiced Maple Syrup

We like to add some delicious aromatics to our syrup. It's a simple way to elevate a classic!

MAKES 2 CUPS (500 ML)

2 cups (500 mL) good-quality pure maple syrup

1 cinnamon stick

4 whole cloves

4 whole star anise

1 In a small saucepan, combine the maple syrup, cinnamon, cloves, and star anise. Keep over low heat until the aroma of the spices begins to permeate the air in your kitchen, 15 to 20 minutes (this can brew on low while you're preparing the rest of breakfast).

2 Remove the pan from the heat, and let the mixture steep for an additional 5 minutes. Strain and serve while warm.

AREA 1.27 m

Classic Crêpes

Pancakes have a perfectly classic feel to them that makes them so at home on our menu, but sometimes you need to cook a quick breakfast for a bunch of late-sleeping cottage-dwellers. Having a simple crêpe recipe in your back pocket means you'll always have something delicious to throw together—a beautiful vehicle for maple syrup or even ham, asparagus, and Béchamel Sauce (Page 154), if you're feeling more savoury.

MAKES ABOUT 16 THIN CRÊPES

1¼ cups (300 mL) all-purpose flour
¼ cup (60 mL) granulated sugar
1 tsp (5 mL) sea salt
1 large egg
1¼ cups (300 mL) homogenized (3.25%) milk
2 tbsp (30 mL) salted butter, melted
Pure maple syrup, for serving

1 In a bowl, whisk together the flour, sugar, and salt.

2 In a small bowl, beat the egg. Add it to the flour mixture. While stirring, gradually add the milk. Stir until fully incorporated.

3 Place a crêpe pan over medium-low heat. Melt the butter. Add the melted butter to the batter and stir to combine. You have also now greased your crêpe pan and are ready to cook.

4 Cook one crêpe at a time. Using a ¼ cup (60 mL) ladle, pour some batter into the centre of the pan, and then twist and turn the pan by the handle to spread the batter around the entire edge of the pan to make a nice big, round, thin pancake. Cook until small bubbles appear through the crêpe and the top turns matte. Flip the crêpe, and cook for about 1 minute on the other side. Fold your crêpe into four, and transfer to a warm plate. Cover with a clean kitchen towel, and repeat with the remaining batter.

5 Enjoy simply with maple syrup or any number of various savoury combinations.

Desserts

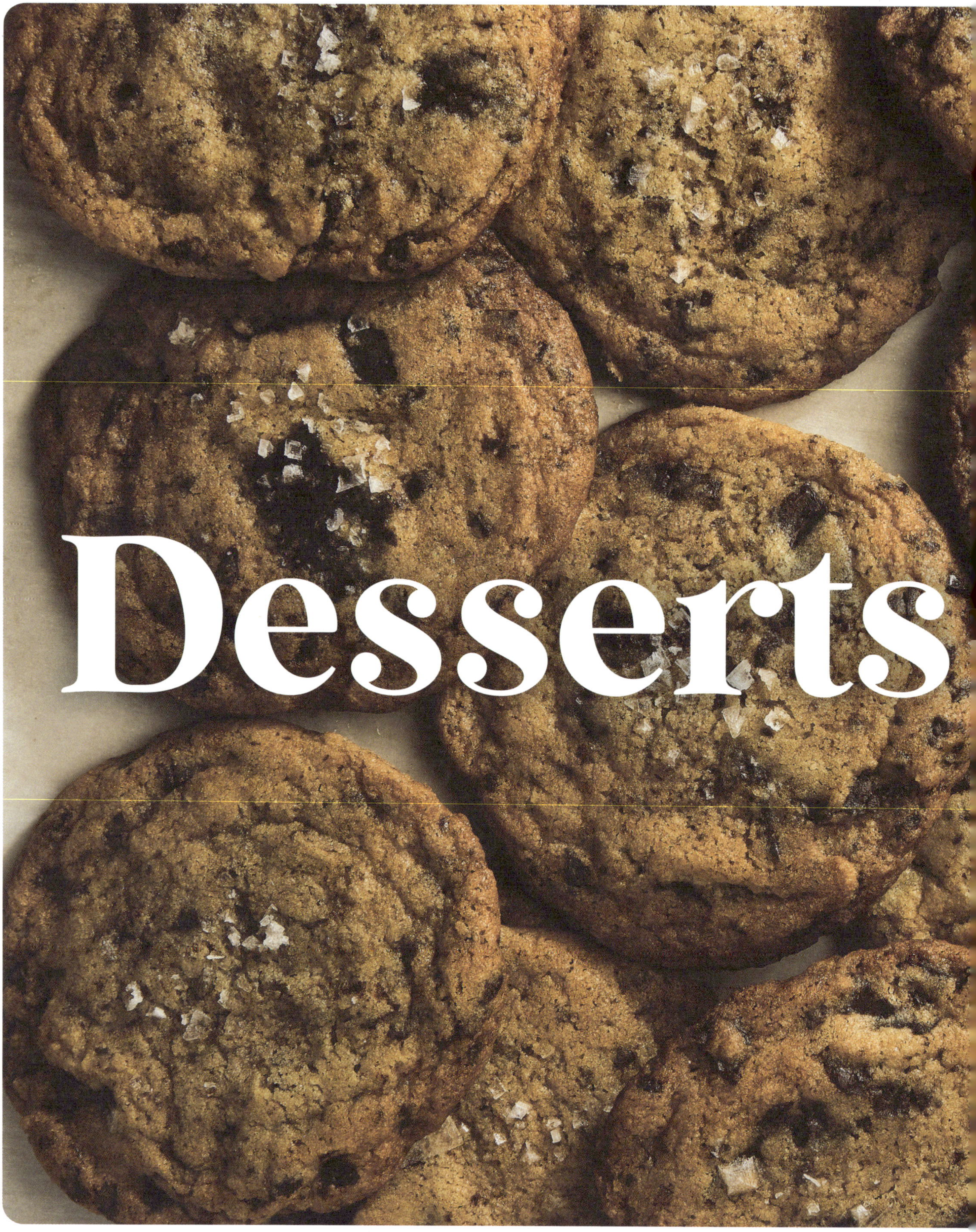

As you will quickly discover, we're pretty darn good at savoury flavours, so you'll find them even in our desserts. We add a little salt just about everywhere because we think it offsets the sweet in a way that makes all our desserts just that much more delectable.

We experimented for a while before we settled on the dessert options that currently grace our menu: the "Key" Lime Parfait (page 265) and the Chocolate Malted Milkshake (page 271). We also tried a bunch of other options along the way that gave us a lot of joy (see the Chocolate-Dipped Frozen Bananas, page 272).

You may not think you have room for dessert, but you do. A wise woman once told us: There is always room on the dessert shelf, even if the appetizer and main course shelves have been filled.

DESSERTS

Heydays Classic Sundae

For a little while, our dessert was the Classic Sundae. We veer away from the "classic" slightly by introducing a delicious oat crumble on top and making sure there's a little bit of salt added to the fudge sauce.

MAKES FIXIN'S FOR 6 TO 8 SUNDAES

Vanilla ice cream
Hot Fudge Sauce (page 262)
Berry Compote (page 262)
Grandmaman's Famous Oats (page 263)
8 oz (225 g) can of whipped cream

1 Scoop out three scoops of vanilla ice cream in a long dish. We like to top the two outside scoops with fudge and the middle one with compote. Top them all with a generous sprinkling of Grandmaman's Famous Oats, and then a dollop of whipped cream. Enjoy!

Hot Fudge Sauce

Certain things are non-negotiable when it comes to ice cream sundaes, and one of them is fudge. We keep this recipe simple, if a little savoury, and pour liberally over our sundaes.

MAKES 1 JAR OF FUDGE (SAVE THE REST IN THE FRIDGE FOR LATER)

¾ cup (175 mL) granulated sugar
½ cup (125 mL) unsweetened cocoa powder
½ cup (125 mL) heavy (whipping) cream
¼ cup (60 mL) salted butter, melted
½ tsp (2 mL) sea salt
½ tsp (2 mL) pure vanilla extract

1 In a medium pot, off the heat, stir together the sugar, cocoa powder, and heavy cream until smooth. Set aside.

2 In a small pot, melt the butter. Pour the melted butter into the cocoa mixture and stir well. Then add the sea salt and vanilla. Place the pan over medium heat. Cook, stirring continuously, until a few simmering bubbles form. Remove the fudge from the heat. Keep in a hot water bath until you are ready to serve.

3 We recommend making this just before you're ready to serve, but it can be refrigerated for up to week and reheated in a hot water bath.

Berry Compote

While we love making this at the height of fresh berry season, it works well with frozen berries, too. It's an easy way to add a bright splash of flavour to desserts, and we're perfectly happy to just spoon it over vanilla ice cream on its own.

MAKES 1½ CUPS (375 ML)

2 cups (500 mL) mixed frozen berries (strawberries, blueberries, raspberries)
3 tbsp (45 mL) granulated sugar
3 tbsp (45 mL) orange juice

1 In a large pot, combine the berries, sugar, and orange juice. Bring the mixture to a simmer over medium heat. Cook until everything looks shiny, about 10 minutes. Remove the pan from the heat, and let sit for 10 minutes. Pour the berry mixture into a blender, and purée until smooth. Strain through a fine-mesh sieve into a bowl or jar. Refrigerate until ready to serve, or up to a week.

Grandmaman's Famous Oats

Freddy's grandmaman was well known for her apple crisp recipe. She worked in a lab, was meticulously clean, and had the ability to slice apples with scientific precision, all a uniform thickness. They were then perfectly laid out in an even pattern at the bottom of the crumble dish. The topping, however, is what made the apple crisp absolutely addictive. We loved it so much, we started sautéing this oat crumble to heap over vanilla ice cream when we didn't have the time to slice apples in a way that would make Grandmaman proud. We loved these oats so much we decided to add them to our sundae.

MAKES 1 CUP (250 ML), OR ENOUGH FOR 6 TO 8 SUNDAES

3 tbsp (45 mL) salted butter (see Heydays Tip)
1 cup (250 mL) large-flake rolled oats (not instant)
2 tbsp (30 mL) brown sugar
½ tsp (2 mL) ground cinnamon

1 In a pan over medium heat, melt the butter. Add the oats, brown sugar, and cinnamon, and then sauté until the oats are slightly crispy. We serve them warm.

Heydays Tip

We always prefer salted butter but especially in desserts where a savoury element adds such addictive complexity to the sweet!

"Key" Lime Parfait

We abandoned the Heydays Classic Sundae (page 261) because it became a lot of work to assemble, which can be hard at the height of our summer season. We looked for something that was very easy to prepare in advance, and Emma discovered a winner—needing only a layer of crumble and a shot of whipped cream to serve. People have absolutely adored this dessert. We almost don't want to admit how simple it is. It's perfectly summery and makes our patio feel like an especially magical, tropical place. Serve a small portion in champagne coupes for a Heydays touch!

SERVES 6

Cream Cheese Filling

2 cups (500 mL) full-fat (33%) cream cheese, softened (2 packages)

2 x 10-oz (300 mL) cans sweetened condensed milk

2 tbsp (30 mL) lime zest

1¼ cups (300 mL) fresh lime juice (real talk: we sometimes use bottled lime juice in a pinch or half lime juice and half lemon)

Crust

(You will have leftovers. Freeze and save for the next time!)

1½ cups (375 mL) crushed honey graham crackers (about 8 crackers)

1½ cups (375 mL) salted pretzels, blended in food processor until crumbs with slight texture

¾ cup (175 mL) granulated sugar

1 cup (250 mL) unsalted butter, melted

½ cup (125 mL) unsweetened shredded dried coconut (optional)

1 tbsp (15 mL) kosher salt

Whipped Cream

2 cups (500 mL) heavy (whipping) cream

1 tsp (5 mL) pure vanilla extract

MAKE THE FILLING

1 In a blender or food processor, combine the cream cheese, condensed milk, and most of the lime zest and juice. (Reserve some lime zest for garnish at the end.) Blend until very smooth. Transfer the mixture to your jars or cups of choice, filling one-third to one-half full. Cover and refrigerate for 4 to 6 hours or overnight.

MAKE THE CRUST

1. Preheat your oven to 400°F (200°C). Line a baking sheet with parchment paper.

2. In a large bowl, stir together the graham crumbs, crushed pretzels, sugar, butter, coconut, and salt. Spread over the prepared baking sheet.

3. Bake in the oven, stirring occasionally, until golden brown, 15–20 minutes.

WHIP THE CREAM

1. In a mixing bowl, combine the cream and the vanilla. Whip until stiff peaks form.

ASSEMBLE

1. Take the key lime base jar out of the fridge. Top with ½ cup (125 mL) of the crust and a generous amount of whipped cream. Sprinkle with the lime zest and enjoy!

Heydays Chocolate Chip Cookies

These cookies end up getting thin and deliciously crispy. We find that chocolate chips don't melt the same way that the chopped chocolate does, resulting in melted shards of chocolate throughout the thin buttery cookie. It wouldn't be a Heydays dessert without a sprinkle of Maldon Salt in there somewhere. We highly recommend it on all your cookies.

MAKES 24 LARGE COOKIES

2½ cups (625 mL) unbleached all-purpose flour
1¼ tsp (6 mL) baking soda
1¼ tsp (6 mL) sea salt
1 cup (250 mL) unsalted butter, at room temperature (we recommend a high-quality butter here—you can really taste it)
2 tsp (10 mL) pure vanilla extract
1 cup (250 mL) granulated sugar
1 cup (250 mL) packed light brown sugar
2 large eggs, at room temperature
2 cups (500 mL) roughly chopped dark chocolate (we like to use a Lindt chocolate bar, but chips are great, too!)
Maldon Salt, for finishing

1. Preheat your oven to 350°F (180°C). Line two or more baking sheets with parchment paper (we space the cookies out on the baking sheets because these babies spread).

2. In a bowl, whisk together the flour, baking soda, and sea salt. Set aside.

3. In the bowl of a stand mixer fitted with the paddle attachment, cream together the butter and vanilla on medium-high speed. Add both sugars, and continue to mix on medium speed until very light and fluffy, about 5 minutes.

4. Add the eggs, and mix no more than 1 minute (they won't fully incorporate into the butter mixture).

5. Reduce the speed to low and gradually incorporate the flour mixture until just combined. Add the chocolate and mix just until incorporated.

6. Using an ice cream scoop or ⅓ cup (75 mL) measure, form the batter into balls and place on the baking sheets, spacing 3 inches (8 cm) apart. Using your fingers, lightly press down on each cookie. Top each cookie with a little sprinkle of Maldon Salt.

7. Bake the cookies, one sheet at a time (yes, it's necessary), in your hot oven for 15 to 19 minutes, until the cookies are (cont'd)

light-medium brown and still soft (they will continue to cook on the baking sheet as they cool). Let them cool on the baking sheet.

8 Store in a resealable container at room temperature for up to a week. Enjoy on their own or as an ice cream sandwich (recipe follows).

Ice Cream Sandwiches

It's a simple one, but we highly recommend using our Chocolate Chip Cookies to make ice cream sandwiches. They were our dessert of choice for a time!

MAKES 12 SANDWICHES

24 Heydays Chocolate Chip Cookies
6 cups (1.5 L) ice cream of your choice

1 Scoop ½ cup (125 mL) of the ice cream of your choice onto the bottom side of one cookie (we love the way vanilla ice cream tastes with the Maldon Salt topping on the cookie). Then top with a second cookie to make your sandwich. Pop the ice cream sandwich into the freezer until you're ready to serve—if the ice cream is too soft, it will just squish out the sides.

Chocolate Malted Milkshake

The summer we brought the Key Lime Parfait onto the menu we knew we'd still need something to satisfy the chocolate lovers, so we created a chocolate malted milkshake. It also happened that one of our other restaurants came with a milkshake machine. Sometimes it's the equipment that has the final say. Malt powder was harder to find than expected, so ultimately we just used malted chocolate balls both in the milkshake and crushed on top, usually with a dash of whipped cream.

MAKES 1 MILKSHAKE

2 scoops of good-quality chocolate ice cream
1 cup (250 mL) homogenized (3.25%) milk
15 malted chocolate balls
Canned whipped cream

1. In a blender, combine the ice cream and milk. Blend until smooth.
2. Add 10 of the malted chocolate balls to the blender, and blend for 3 seconds, until the malt balls are crushed but you can still see chunks.
3. Pour the milkshake into your desired cup. Top with a swirl of whipped cream.
4. Place the remaining 5 malted chocolate balls in a resealable bag, seal, and crush them. Sprinkle the crushed malt balls on top of the whipped cream. Enjoy!

Chocolate-Dipped Frozen Bananas

We were looking for an easy made-in-advance dessert and took inspiration from one of our favourite television shows. If you know, you know. It's a fun dessert to have on hand. And besides, what could a banana possibly cost?

MAKES 6 HALF BANANAS

3 bananas with yellow skin (no brown spotted ones!), peeled and halved widthwise
6 popsicle sticks
1 cup (250 mL) chopped dark chocolate
½ cup (125 mL) finely chopped nuts (peanuts, pistachios, or walnuts)
Your choice of toppings (see Heydays Tip)

1. Line a baking sheet with parchment paper. Make sure you have room in your freezer to place it.

2. Insert the popsicle sticks into the cut side of the banana, half way down the middle, and place on your prepared baking sheet. Freeze until firm, about 2 hours.

3. Melt the chocolate in a 2-cup (500 mL) glass measuring pitcher or anything that the bananas can easily be dipped into. Melt the chocolate in the microwave in 30-second intervals until smooth.

4. Working quickly, dip the frozen bananas into the melted chocolate until each one is fully covered, using a spoon to scrape off any excess. Place the chocolate-coated banana back on the parchment-lined baking sheet and sprinkle with nuts. Do this as each banana is dipped, or the chocolate will set from the cold banana and your nuts won't stick!

5. Return all 6 bananas to the freezer and leave for 15 minutes to set. Once set they can be stored in a resealable container for up to a week.

Heydays Tip

Feel free to get creative with toppings. Think coconut, sprinkles, or crushed-up chocolate candies.

Heydays Classic Cheesecake

Rich. Decadent. Classic. That's where most of our menu lands when it comes to adjectives, so that's how we'll finish. This recipe is a little longer and has some steps beyond your average cheesecake, but it makes it worth it. In typical Heydays fashion, we add something savoury to the crust to get a true balance of flavours. If you can use a scale, please do!

MAKES ONE 9-INCH (23 CM) CHEESECAKE

For the crust:

1 cup (250 mL) graham crumbs
1 cup (250 mL) crushed pretzels
2 tbsp (30 mL) salted butter, melted
1 tsp (5 mL) kosher salt

For the filling:

4 x 32-oz (900 g) packages full-fat (33%) cream cheese, softened
10½ oz (300 g) full-fat (20%) goat's cheese
1 tbsp (15 mL) pure vanilla extract
1 tbsp (15 mL) fresh lemon juice
1 tsp (5 mL) kosher salt
¾ cup (175 mL) heavy (whipping) cream
1½ cups (375 mL) granulated sugar
6 large eggs, whisked

MAKE THE CRUST:

1 Preheat your oven to 450°F (230°C). Line the bottom of a 9-inch (23 cm) springform pan with parchment paper.

2 In a bowl, using your hands, combine the graham crumbs, pretzels, salt, and butter. Press into the bottom of the springform pan. Set aside.

MAKE THE FILLING:

1 In a stand mixer fitted with the paddle attachment, on medium speed, beat the softened cream cheese, goat's cheese, vanilla, lemon juice, and salt until smooth and creamy, about 3 minutes. (Alternatively, use a bowl and hand mixer.) Using a spatula, scrape down the sides of the bowl and mix for an additional 2 minutes, until you reach a lump-free, creamy mixture.

2 Meanwhile, in a small saucepan, heat the cream until just boiling. Set aside.

3 Stop the mixer, and then add the sugar all at once. Blend until combined. Once the sugar is combined, take the bowl off the stand and set a fine-mesh sieve on top of the bowl. Pour the mixed eggs into the sieve over the cream cheese mixture, and whisk until the eggs have passed through the sieve (there will be clumps of eggs that don't make it through, and that is (cont'd)

what you want). Put the bowl back onto the stand and mix until just combined.

4 Pour the heated cream mixture into the eggy cream cheese mixture (the heat from the cream helps remove any bubbles in the cheesecake while it bakes).

5 Place the springform pan onto a baking sheet, and then pour the cream cheese mixture over the unbaked graham crust. Bake in your hot oven for 20 minutes, until the cake puffs up and turns slightly brown, creating flavour.

6 Reduce the oven temperature to 250°F (120°C) and bake for another 45 to 60 minutes, until the cheesecake reads 150°F (65°C) when a thermometer is inserted into the middle and the cake has about 2 inches (5 cm) of wiggle in the middle when slightly jiggled.

7 Remove the cheesecake from the oven and let cool for 15 minutes. Then run a knife around the edge of the cake to help release it from the pan. Continue to cool at room temperature for 3 to 4 hours before putting it in your fridge overnight (or for at least 10 hours) to firm up.

8 Enjoy this cheesecake plain, with chocolate or caramel sauce, or, our personal favourite, with a fresh seasonal Berry Compote (page 262).

How It's Going

After four successful seasons in Heydays at The June Motel, our favourite thing is still our regulars. We've met people who have visited The June four years in a row, and we have seasonal locals who have been coming almost every week since we started in the parking lot. Their loyalty and support astound us. We love all our guests, but we take special joy in seeing our regulars and try to make each experience better than the last.

It is the great challenge of the hospitality industry.

April and Sarah continue to be on the lookout for the next perfect motel property, and when they find it, there may very well be space for another Heydays. We can't wait to see where the next adventure takes us.

Acknowledgements

We first have to thank the guests who took a chance on a restaurant in a parking lot in 2020 and have been coming back ever since—we wouldn't be here without you. Motel guests, seasonal cottagers, and year-round locals have made Heydays their own. We are so grateful that you choose our patio for your special moments, and we are happy to call you our friends.

Thank you to our incredible staff, who take care of our guests every day. It can be a hard job at the height of our busy summers, but you keep this whole thing afloat and make it fun in the process! Our guests come for the food, but they stay for the wonderful people who work at Heydays. Rob, thank you for elevating our service from day one (under a face shield while getting paid in wine). Angelia, from year one dishwasher to running the kitchen, thank you! Chef Tyler Cunningham, we're so grateful you came aboard. To Supachai and Johnny: Thank you for bringing your incredible skills, positivity, and kindness to our kitchen.

To April and Sarah: Thank you for including us in this wild journey. It has been a life-changing experience that we couldn't possibly have foreseen when we first met. It has been such a pleasure to grow with you, and we are, as always, excited for all that is to come!

We joined an incredible community in Sauble Beach. We're so grateful for our fellow business owners, the Sauble Seagulls, the Sauble Beach Chamber of Commerce, and all the people who have supported us along the way, especially Lori Brierley, Sam Driver, Justine Jackson, and Chantelle Riberdy—you keep us going! Local suppliers like Dave Fretz, Kevin at North Sauble Meats and More, Kevin at Howell's, Bill from Bill's Produce, Sean from Kolapore Springs, and Hi-Berry Farms keep great products in our kitchen all summer long.

To the Knight family: Your legacy lives on, and we strive every day to live up to it. We are so thrilled every time we see you on the patio your family built. Thank you.

Thank you to Doug Richmond for serendipitously coming to Sauble Beach in 2020 and deciding to take on this project. We are so grateful for you and the whole team at Anansi, including Michelle MacAleese, Jenny McWha, Greg Tabor, Karen Brochu, Semareh Al-Hillal, Laura Chapnick, Tracy Bordian, and Janice Weaver. Thank you for all your patience with us as we navigated the publishing world during the busy season. We are so happy to be working with you.

Abundant thanks to our creative partners: To Jackie Treitz, our brilliant designer, thank you for building such a beautiful brand and for all your insights throughout this process. To Lauren Miller, our amazing photographer, your photos made us believe we could make a cookbook to begin with! To Rayna Marlee Schwartz, you added organization and flair to our chaos—thank you. To Courtney Mann, thank you for everything, but we are especially grateful for this last creative project with you. To Paige Bush and Shelby Hiscock, for all the photo shoot coordination and support. To Penny Light at Grit & Grace, thank you for supplying wardrobe for the photo shoot and for being such an amazing friend. To all our wonderful models, thank you for making cold days in May look like fun!

Many thanks to the dear writing friends who read early drafts of this book, especially Jade, Lori, Melissa, Oscar, and Shari, and fellow attendees of workshops at Firefly Creative Writing and Carmel Futures. Thank you to Jesse, Lucie, and Rose for sharing your publishing knowledge and travelling many hours (many times over) to eat at our restaurant!

Thank you to Steven and Diane, Nicola and Art, Mary Beth and Jim, Marina and Serge, and all of our siblings and their partners—we wouldn't be able to do this without your love and support!

Heydays
OYSTERS $2/GO $3/STAY
CHARRED BROCCOLI CAESAR $11
LOBSTER BISQUE $11 SOLD OUT
CLASSIC MAC + CHEESE $11 (V) SOLD OUT
LOBSTER MAC + CHEESE $22 SOLD OUT
OLD BAY FRIED CHICKEN $17
HOT LOBSTER ROLL $20
SMASH BURGER $13.50
BEYOND BRAT $14 (VG)
FRESH CUT FRIES $4 (VG)
VEG OF THE DAY $7 (VG)
PAN SEARED TROUT + LENTILS $24
Something Sweet
BEACH ICE CREAM SANDWICH $7
VANILLA ICE CREAM, CHOCOLATE CHIP COOKIE, PEANUTS

RECIPE INDEX

Page numbers in italic indicate photos.

About the Authors

FREDDY LALIBERTÉ opened numerous food concepts in Toronto prior to relocating to Sauble Beach to open Heydays. He researched and developed recipes for the hard-hitting classics that customers keep coming back for, and specializes in sourcing excellent products and keeping quality high in all our Heydays dishes.

EVAN BAULCH is an operational mastermind in charge of pulling all the pieces of complex restaurant operations together and keeping things running smoothly day to day. His vast experience in high-end hospitality establishments in Toronto and the Guelph area helped him to develop the practices that weave rhythm, routine, and consistency in all that we do.

KATIE LALIBERTÉ spent weekends in 2020 working the Heydays patio and leverages her day-job skills to support all the tech systems that make up a busy restaurant. She's a writer and sometime bookseller, and is currently working on a restaurant romance!

EMMA BAULCH has long been known for her tastemaking culinary prowess and is now responsible for finding and hiring our staff, creating the best hospitality teams in Bruce County. She is our queen of desserts and our forever HR expert.

Someday
these will
be the good
old days